REMEMBER
ME AS
HUMAN

REMEMBER
ME AS
HUMAN

What Three Final Days with My Grandmother
Wanda Taught Me about Truly Living

A MEMOIR BY
LUCY WALSH

PARTING GLASS PUBLISHING
Los Angeles, California

REMEMBER ME AS HUMAN

What Three Final Days with My Grandmother
Wanda Taught Me about Truly Living

A memoir by Lucy Walsh

This book is a memoir. It reflects my present recollections of experiences over years of time. I have done my best to make it tell a truthful story; therefore, no names have been changed, nor characters invented. I would like to thank living members of my family portrayed in this book for helping me with facts and dates. I recognize that their memories of the events described may be different from my own.

Cover design by Drew Foerster
Interior design by Gilman Design, Larkspur, Calif.

Photo Credits:
Author photo, Justin Picarri
All other photos courtesy of the Lucy Walsh Family Collection

DEDICATION

For my mother Jody. We're all both miracles.

And to my readers.
May we have the courage to be fully human
while we're alive.
May we be remembered as human after we're gone.

Worship the ground your loved ones walk on, hon,
because it's a long road without them.
– Wanda Mae Boyer

FAMILY TREE
⟶ WANDA & DALE ⟵

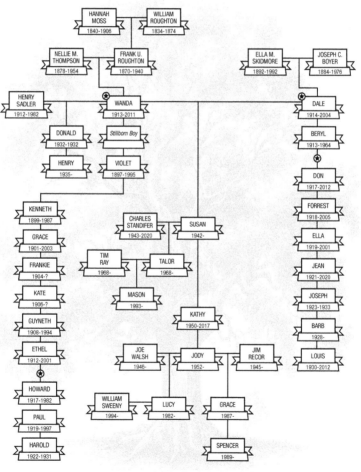

HANNAH MOSS 1840-1906 — WILLIAM ROUGHTON 1834-1874

NELLIE M. THOMPSON 1878-1954 — FRANK U. ROUGHTON 1870-1940

ELLA M. SKIDMORE 1892-1992 — JOSEPH C. BOYER 1884-1976

HENRY SADLER 1912-1982 — ⭐ WANDA 1913-2011

⭐ DALE 1914-2004

DONALD 1932-1932 — Stillborn Boy

BERYL 1913-1964

HENRY 1935- — VIOLET 1897-1995

⭐ DON 1917-2012

KENNETH 1899-1987

FORREST 1918-2005

GRACE 1901-2003

CHARLES STANDIFER 1943-2020 — SUSAN 1942-

ELLA 1919-2001

FRANKIE 1904-?

TIM RAY 1968- — TALOR 1968-

JEAN 1921-2020

KATE 1906-?

MASON 1993-

JOSEPH 1923-1933

GUYNETH 1908-1994

KATHY 1950-2017

BARB 1928-

ETHEL 1912-2001

JOE WALSH 1946- — JODY 1952- — JIM RECOR 1945-

LOUIS 1930-2012

⭐ HOWARD 1917-1982

WILLIAM SWEENY 1994- — LUCY 1982- — GRACE 1987-

PAUL 1919-1997

HAROLD 1922-1931

SPENCER 1989-

CONTENTS

NOT THE FIRST CHAPTER

IF YOU'RE LIKE ME, you occasionally skip over Introductions. I know, I know; very bad reader manners, and I feel terrible writing it out loud, but I admit it! I used to think Introductions were unimportant fluff, keeping me from getting straight to the story. That was before… before I wrote a book myself. Now I understand their purpose: to set up the story, to give you crucial background on what you're about to read. But since you may still feel like I used to, I'm not calling this an Introduction. You're already in, baby.

In 2000, when I was seventeen years old, my grandmother sat me down on the botanical-garden-print couch in her home in Urbana, Illinois, one summer afternoon and said she had a very special gift for me. That moment is such a clear snapshot in my memory: the stifling orange sun radiating through the room's one small window, illuminating dust specks in the air and heating the worn corduroy armchairs; the upholstered couch where we sat; my grandma's prized spinet organ, where she'd taught me to sing harmonies as a kid. The house had been built in 1878; my grandparents Wanda and Dale Boyer bought it as newlyweds in 1940 and raised their four children there: Henry, Susie, Kathy, and Jody (my mom). That it could've boasted three bedrooms in just nine hundred and fifty square feet seems implausible, but it snugly did.

My whole life, my mom had flown us from our

home in Los Angeles for visits several times a year. With us was always my "Jim Dad," her husband since I was three, and later my younger (half-) siblings, Grace and Spencer. Those family trips to my mom's birth home and the surrounding idyllic country towns full of relatives always excited me deeply—everything so drastically different from my life in L.A.

That hot summer day in 2000, Grandma Wanda rose from the couch and opened the living room closet, pulling down from a high shelf what she told me was her most cherished possession: the sixty-three remaining letters that my Grandfather Dale had written to her during the three years he served as a corporal in World War II. I rose as she handed them to me in a tattered plastic grocery bag; my mouth fell open and my eyes widened in surprise. I tried to carefully take them but more like excitedly snatched them from her and held them to my chest, speechless. I couldn't believe they were mine to keep, but she said she wanted me to have them and that it was time. I don't know why, out of everyone in our family, she chose me, but I'm so grateful, because in many ways it has guided the course of my life. I think heirlooms find their way to the person who will protect them best.

As we stood there, Wanda showed me how Dale had begun and ended every single letter to her in the same way: his signature opening "Hello My Darling" and his eternal signoff "With all my love and kisses, Your Husband." During their long separation, Dale had sent three times as many letters, but over the fifty-five years since the war, many had been misplaced. The sixty-three surviving letters had been written over a span of just seven months, from July 3, 1944, to February 6, 1945 —a brief and priceless peek at one dynamic couple's relationship during an extraordinary moment in history.

When I wondered where Wanda's replies were, she told me that not one of her several hundred return letters had survived the war. Dale describes in one letter having to burn hers along the way, because his infantry unit was constantly moving just behind the front lines in France, and he was unable to hang on to any excess weight. From a letter dated July 6, 1944: "There's one thing I really hate to do and that is to burn all your lovely letters my dear. I have two big boxes of them and I can't say how much each one of them has meant to me."

I'd give anything to have her letters to pair with his, but some things in life are destined to live only in our imagination. I have spent many hours painstakingly time-lining Dale's letters and filling in the blanks to questions such as "You told me you went to the dentist, how's the tooth?" or "How was your trip down to your parent's farm?" with what her responses might have been. Improvising Wanda's answers achieves a semblance of their conversation, at least. But it's not even a shadow of what was.

As soon as I accepted the letters, they presented me with a world of creative possibility. As a professional actor, writer, and musician, I've built a career creating tangible things from my experiences. Alchemy is what it is. Even at seventeen, before I had a career, my mind went there, and I began hatching a project about the letters on the largest scale I could imagine: a Ron Howard film, of course. But how on earth was I to go about making that happen? For the rest of my teens, I day-dreamed about waiting outside Mr. Howard's office with my ratty plastic bag of old letters, a passionate young wanna-be pitching him my epic World War II love story as he hurried to his car.

I didn't have any sense of a plot at that point, not a single word of a story, but he as the filmmaker was cemented in my mind. My daydreams involved carrying the letters in my purse at all times (which I literally did)—so maybe if I ran into Mr. Howard at the grocery store, I could pitch him the story as we browsed the canned goods together, his hand holding his garden peas in mid-air, so transfixed was he by the story.

The late, legendary director Garry Marshall later described these chance parking lot and grocery store meetings to me as "bump-ins," saying that some of his most successful television and film projects had begun this way. Though I didn't know there was a term for it back when I was an aspiring teenager, a chance run-in with Mr. Howard seemed my best plan of success for the letters making it to the big screen, as I knew they were destined to. (If that younger Lucy could have foreseen that she would actually get her chance to share the story with Mr. Howard one day, she would've melted into a puddle of happiness.)

As this strategizing carried me into my early twenties, my Grandfather Dale died of Alzheimer's disease before I got a chance to begin asking him anything personal. I hadn't had the wherewithal to ask him the things I now desperately wish I knew about his life, his letters, the war. I've been pretty beat up by that regret, both for myself and for the research toward a film about him. I have to remind myself that he was not talkative to begin with, and getting him to open up had always been like trying to juice a stone.

The horror of losing my grandpa to Alzheimer's was major for me. I watched him forget everything and everyone he knew. Before Dale's slow demise, I had always regarded death as the thief of life in one fell swoop, mind and body taken all at once. But this was totally different; here, death played filthy dirty and stole my loved one's mind long before his body, while his life was still in full swing.

Once Grandpa died, in 2004, I felt compelled on a whole new level to someday, somehow, make his letters the basis of a film, and my purpose became crystal clear: I would bring Grandpa's memories back, and I would pass them on so that no one ever forgot. That dream proved my way of working through the pain of watching his memory ripped from him before my eyes.

I also worried that Alzheimer's might strike someone else close to me. I went into overdrive asking questions of not only elders but everyone around me. Parents, aunts, uncles, my two remaining grandparents, my siblings and friends—I had to gather everybody's memories. That way, Alzheimer's could never win. The disease was a major catalyst for my interviewing my grandmother about her life, and subsequently this book.

Actually, I have always been a people historian, fascinated with asking others what their lives have been like and preserving their answers in my journals. In grade school, I'd spend recess up in a tree, observing and cataloging my peers' interactions in the yard below. What I was collecting others' experiences and movements for, I never knew, but now I think I understand more about where it was coming from. My beautiful mom, Jody Boyer, and musician dad, Joe Walsh, were together for eleven years but divorced just after I was born; this must have been an attempt to piece together a firmer foundation, a stronger, wider sense of family, as I grew up.

A FEW MONTHS AFTER Dale's death, Wanda phoned my mom to say she was ready to move to a nursing home. No, she insisted, she did not want to move in with one of her children. She left behind seventy years of her life in Urbana and relocated forty-five minutes away to the Boxwood Nursing Home, where Dale had lived the last few years of his life. She took with her only the essentials: her clothes, her armchair, and her electric keyboard.

During those first years after Wanda entered the nursing home, I was very busy as a touring musician, and I didn't see her or call very often. I was having incredible experiences, performing my music all over the world, so my head drifted away from creating a film for a solid chunk of my twenties. A project was always in the back of my mind, but I accepted it as a beautiful fantasy that was simply too lofty to achieve. Six wild years passed.

It wasn't until 2010, after I'd made the decision to stop the touring life and stay in L.A. to focus on acting, that I began speaking with Grandma Wanda more regularly, calling her every few weeks. The moment I turned back to acting, ideas for the film began calling my name again. As I took the letters from their long sleep in a drawer and began to read them again, Dale's words posed newly realized questions I needed answers to, answers only Wanda could give now. So I would pepper our every phone conversation with a few of them, coaxing her to share in depth the stories I'd heard about her, things the letters alluded to; but she never seemed to want to speak much about her life.

What she did want to speak about, constantly, was her deepening longing to be reunited with her mother and ten siblings. She was the very last one still alive of eleven brothers and sisters, her parents, her beloved husband, and her heart was understandably more on the other side with them than it was here in the physical world. I could feel a growing race against mortality itself to gather her memories, and after my painful lesson in losing Grandpa, I knew better than to take this window of time for granted. Kicking myself for having let life get in the way for too long already, I made a plan to talk with her in person. I wanted an official sit-down interview with Wanda, no more dodging questions.

Meantime, while Wanda was becoming so fixated on dying, the fates threw me a curveball: Her doctor began overmedicating her. As she was prescribed multiple medications and naively taking them, she began to disappear into a stranger. Just like Grandpa. For three months, we really thought we had lost her as she forgot who she was, became incoherent at times, overly emotional to the point of weepy hysteria, even telling my mom, "I just want to go stand on the highway and let a car hit me."

This was not Wanda; this was depressants talking, and my mom took action. Mom ordered the doctors to eliminate all but Wanda's necessary meds and not to give her so much as an aspirin without asking. They obeyed, and Wanda came back to us. This close call was the last straw for me—no more procrastinating; it was time to go to her.

In January of 2011, I sat with my Grandmother Wanda Mae Boyer in her nursing home and interviewed her on camera about her ninety-seven-year-long life. This book is the story of those three days with Wanda, including the people and events that informed them, from our ancestors in England to the residents in her nursing home. Wanda was completely unaware of having any lessons of value to offer anyone, and yet she has been one of my greatest teachers. Wanda taught me what it is to be fully human; to embrace our human experience with dignity and courage, even though we know it will end. Her story, yes, but inevitably mine, too. And I share it with you now, with all my love, because I know that this ache to wholly understand ourselves through where and who we have come from is our deepest common thread.

CHAPTER ONE

WHEN I CALLED TO tell Grandma Wanda I was coming to see her in a few days, she excitedly yelped into the phone. I said I hoped to speak with her on camera about her long life, trying to spell it out for her simply, like explaining it to a child. This was a woman who could not fathom the point of sharing the intimate details of one's life or getting warm and fuzzy about feelings. She was a proud, foul-mouthed old clucker—*snarky*, as she put it. *Snarky* was one of her favorite words.

A dictionary definition of *snarky* is "Sharply critical; cutting, snide." Wanda was all those things, although never mean-spirited. Her personality was without shame, bubbling over with witty home-cooked humor, seasoned with back-country slang that doesn't even exist anymore.

On that initial phone call, she said flat out that she did not want to be interviewed. No, no, no. She would definitely like me to come for a visit, please—no questions about personal stuff, though, and definitely no camera. Her immediate resistance was not a surprise to me; I had fully expected her to buck against this foreign event trying to force its way into her routine at this late stage in her life. While she spoke so loudly into the phone that the sound distorted, my brain was churning with new ways of approaching her to get what I wanted and needed.

As my flight loomed, I continued to call her and pitch

the situation. I even dangled incentives like foot rubs and treats from her favorite ice-cream parlor; and after more promised foot rubs than I could possibly deliver in a lifetime, I finally got her to agree to "a chat." I could make a chat work! She still insisted that she didn't want any cameras there, so I stopped mentioning that part for now. I'd cross that bridge when I came to it.

With the YES from Wanda in place and my flight leaving the next day, I was down to the wire in preparing my questions for our chat. I was still focused on asking about specific things written in the letters, but my time away from them had unconsciously broadened my curiosity. I had questions about the beautiful moments in her life, but I also needed to ask about some tough stuff my family had worked hard to sweep under the rug. It was important that I keep Wanda feeling safe, but it felt necessary to ask about everything. Even the one thing. Especially the one thing.

Looking back, I see that I assigned the interview magical qualities and had some pretty surreal expectations about how it would go down. I'd assumed that as Wanda was nearing a century old, she would open up about her life like never before, memories and revelations cascading from her with earth-shattering sentiment. There certainly were revelations lying in wait, just not in the emotional-fireworks way I had imagined. The real revelations were for me, not Wanda. I was in for a master class on what it is to be human.

AS I BOARDED THE midnight flight with just a backpack

of clothes and my camera equipment, I was jittery with excitement and nerves. The stakes were very high in my mind. I took this assignment so seriously, I felt like Anderson Cooper headed to interview the president or something. Amid these ordinary passengers with their wheelies and Cinnabons, I carried an extraordinary assignment, a responsibility to myself, Wanda, and humanity at large. The letters in my bag were a priceless piece of history, after all, which made it necessary to ask Wanda about the stories behind them so that I could turn it into the most epic film of all time, something that would change people's lives. That was my self-appointed mission. No pressure.

Landing in the blue early-morning light of Indianapolis, I collected the keys to a rented gray something-or-other with no bells and absolutely no whistles. Bag and gear thrown onto the back seat, I putted off on the two-hour journey to the Boxwood Nursing Home, in the tiny town of Newman, thirty miles from where Wanda had been born, in Mayview, Illinois.

Her first known ancestor to arrive in the surrounding area of Champaign County was William Roughton, her father's father. The year was 1853, and William was a nineteen-year-old emigrant from England. A ship called the *Wyoming* had carried William across the Atlantic from Liverpool with his fifty-six-year-old mother, Ann Pimm, and a handful of siblings. William's father, Gervase Roughton, had died three years earlier, and the family sought a new start in America. After a grueling thirty-five days at sea, they landed in Philadelphia on

June 13 and dispersed to various parts of the Midwest—
Kentucky, Ohio, Illinois.

At twenty-seven, my Great-Great-Grandfather William
volunteered for service in the American Civil War,
enlisting as a private in 1861, a corporal by the time
of his release two years later. Before he signed up for
the draft, William had fallen in love with Hannah Moss,
a Kentucky woman six years younger. He carried
Hannah's picture in his uniform pocket all through the
fighting, until he was badly wounded at Chickamauga,
Georgia, on September 19, 1863. The injury got William
discharged a year and a half before the war ended, and
he was able to make it back to Hannah. They married
on September 14, 1864. Hannah and I are ancestral
homegirls, if you will; I followed in her footsteps and
became the second American woman in the family to
marry an Englishman named William, one hundred
fifty-six years later.

Although William and Hannah married in her home
state of Kentucky, they settled in Illinois, where he
worked as a mechanic and farmer while she was busy
running the household. Most of the grain towns dotting
these areas were established in the mid-eighteen
hundreds by wealthy landowners in anticipation of the
railroad rolling through. The couple's move to Illinois,
not far from their future Granddaughter Wanda's
present-day nursing home, most likely had to do with
staying close to William's immigration sponsor, who
lived there.

According to the 1870 census (William now thirty-six,
Hannah twenty-nine), they had three children, Allen,

Minora, and Melvin, and, from all accounts, a loving marriage. Their happiness was not destined to last much longer, however, for William died just four years later after he was kicked in the head by a horse.

And instead of the promised progress of the railroads, the land holdings were broken up and sold off as investors fell away. The financiers may have lost interest and left for cities, but my relatives stayed on as farmers and business owners and thrived. Those old railroad lines have been transformed into bike and jogging paths. Now, a hundred and forty-one years after that 1870 census, I was driving through those communities and their invisible forcefield of my ancestor's past to Wanda and our interview.

———

As I crossed the state line with my windows cranked down, the air began to smell of fresh earth, something I was not used to. At home in the Malibu mountains, I knew well the odors of California buckwheat and oak trees, plants like sagebrush and fennel. The smells in Illinois woodland were like from another planet: pungent manure, newly mown hay and grass, lilacs, the sweetness of corn and bean crops, the dampness of wooden barns, the indescribable scent in the air before and after a rainstorm. The Illinois temperatures, too, were thrilling and overwhelming: suffocating heat and gripping cold, unlike the mild, ongoing seventy degrees of coastal California. The wind on my face was freezing, but I had a thick jacket on and drank in the sensation.

Sleeping winter fields stretched as far as I could see on both sides of the road, rich dark soil full of dreaming seeds that would transform into sky-high waves of green corn and rows of shimmering soybeans come summer. Far out on the expanse where land and sky met was the occasional patch of woods: beech, hickory, maple trees. There were not many neighborhoods out here on these country roads, and any town I did encounter I passed through in about four seconds. Here, the world turned at a different pace, and as I fell into the rhythm of the land, I zoomed way over the speed limit and tightened my game plan.

My prior excitement was breaking down into pure nerves, and surges of adrenaline were making me queasy. I was so excited about the experience I was about to dive into with Wanda, but I also felt apprehensive about entering the Boxwood Nursing Home again. This fear was a familiar feeling. I'd visited various relatives here over the years—with my mom and Jim Dad when I was young, then alone as I got older and came through town on music tours. I had always taken an emotional hit from spending time there, even before I was old enough to understand why.

It wasn't only my Grandpa Dale who spent his final years in the "old folks' home," as we called it as kids. Dale had had cousins, aunts, and uncles who had lived in these bright, sterile rooms, even his parents, Clinton and Marie Boyer, before him. From a child's perspective, most of the people seemed lonely, forgotten, as if waiting there to die. There was a hopelessness about the place. It plagued me as a kid; it still does. The faces of those lost people lining the halls on long-ago visits flood my mind if I let them.

As a society, we largely neglect our elderly. We hide them away. Old age is not convenient for our economy; it is clear from our laws that the government would love us to be done living the moment our working years end. But how can we shun old age, withdraw support, lose patience, try to ignore those who've survived so long when it is our own fate? I just answered my own question, actually. We do not like to confront our fate. Our lives are very much designed around obsessively outrunning the reality that we will not always be young and beautiful. Scarlett O'Hara summed it up in *Gone With the Wind* when she remarked, "I won't think about that now…. I'll think about it tomorrow."

GETTING CLOSE NOW. I was just thirty minutes from the nursing home, still surrounded by naked motionless fields, and my thoughts strayed from dark to lighter memories of visiting my grandparents at their home. The city of Urbana, while a busy college town home to the University of Illinois, has averaged a population in my lifetime of thirty-nine thousand people, compared to L.A.'s 3.65 million. The stark difference in the number of people, and the old-fashioned ways of life in the Midwest, have always made me think of Illinois as otherworldly, exotic. It might sound funny to describe a landlocked state as exotic, but coming from the palm trees and brushfires of California, that's how it felt to young me.

Two visits in particular stand out. When I was about eight, we surprised my grandparents at Christmas by pretending to be carolers. As we sang our hearts out just beyond their snowy stoop, their jaws dropped when they realized it was us under the layers of scarves and hats. It was a joyous mess of excited shrieks, hugs, and laughs as they ran down the steps to embrace us.

During our summer visits, the yard would transform into a lush paradise in which fireflies glittered and flitted at dusk. I was obsessed with catching them in a jar, admiring their light for a few moments before releasing them into the air again. Staying with my grandparents one Fourth of July evening, I was a bit freaked out by the loud fireworks I could hear from their stoop. My grandpa held me close and told me the noise was giant elephants walking around in town, just over the trees. WOW, I thought, Illinois truly is magical.

In the snug living room of their tiny castle on the corner of Urbana and California avenues, Dale favored the tan corduroy armchair while Wanda claimed the matching green one, which she always draped with lace doilies on its back and arms. Between them sat the wood-console television set on the floor. The pair sat there like a king and his queen, ruling their mini-kingdom with cans of American beer in their hands.

Wanda, with her lacquered-bubble hairdo (which during my lifetime ran the gamut from natural auburn to dyed Lucille Ball red to Betty White white), always dressed smartly, even when staying home. At night for bed she wore long silk nightgowns in pastels, but during the day she preferred pantsuits in bright colors to anything else. I never saw her in a dress or skirt, although I know from photos that she wore them in her younger years, when it was the accepted female attire.

I adored everything about Grandma—her house, her bedroom, especially her mirrored vanity. She had treasures in the drawers and laid out on lace: perfumes, powders, hairpins, costume jewelry. In the soft glow of the two Victorian milk-glass lamps that lit her face in the mirror, she would show me thrilling things, one at a time. At the vanity we spoke in our special whispers, but out in the living room, she was loud and lively, usually having heated one-sided conversations with the television or barking commands at their daughter Kathy.

With all this raucous life going on around him, Dale just sat quietly in his armchair or out on the glassed-in porch, sipping his beer from the can, lost in silence. Silence. My grandfather taught me silence. His silence made me pay attention to him; it made me feel safe. He listened more than he spoke. I liked sitting near him, but it wasn't for the riveting conversation, that's for sure.

I never knew him with anything but gray hair. I guess Wanda dyed her hair far past the time he lost the natural color in his. He wore the same get-up every day: belted jeans and a button-up shirt with boots. He was a simple man, on the outside anyway.

Although as a child, I had no concept of his inner world, I've learned from his letters that he was deeply romantic and bursting with love for life. He whole-heartedly poured his humor, hopes, fears, and imaginings into his writing with subtle poetic flair. It's strange to have known him as that emotionally reserved old man in his seventies and eighties, then later to discover him as the gushing Romeo of his twenties—very different aspects of one man that never came together in front of me. His voice in his letters is so loud in my head, a good friend I know by heart...but the actual man's voice I barely remember.

What I do remember is being with Grandpa in the woods. Hunting and fishing were his ceremonies. Nature was his religion. Dale moved through life by the cycles of the seasons and was fluent in the language of the earth, no doubt passed down through generations of country living.

I remember the squirrel tails he hung on the trees in the yard after a good hunt as he prepared the little animals. I didn't get to go on his hunting trips, but I did eat the meals afterward, and I have to say, squirrel is delicious. Today, a city woman who buys her meat at a grocery store and thus remains disconnected from the killing process, I would be disturbed to witness the butchering of an adorable animal. But back then I considered it normal, just something my grandpa did, and his grandpa before him.

And I can see the fishing line he cast in the dark waters of Homer Lake—never a bobber, as he preferred to fish off the bottom. I recall one summer visit with my whole family, a beautiful day of green velvet earth and crisp blue sky crowded with billowing white clouds. We don't have days like that in Los Angeles, the smog would never allow it. Grandpa was teaching five-year-old Spencer how to fish as Grace haphazardly swished her pole around her head; my mom laughed and helped, while Jim Dad sat back and smiled. I considered myself quite my grandfather's protégé and insisted I could handle my pole alone.

Once Spencer lost interest, Grandpa cast his line out into the water, dug the pole into the bank, and wandered into the woods to walk alone, beer can in hand. Whenever he did this, he had a fish hooked when he returned. This was a constant annoyance to Grandma, who, my mom says, on the rare occasions she came along to fish with Dale, stayed glued to the water's edge with her eyes on her line to detect the slightest nibble, which she rarely got. Normally, she preferred to go out to play Bingo or stay home with my Aunt Kathy.

Kathy was my mom's older sister by seventeen months. She was born with special needs, as we say now—it was called "mental retardation" or simply "retarded" back then. Wanda and Dale were truly the exception during that era, when many children like Kathy were sent away to institutions, and they didn't take that advice. After her diagnosis at age five, they kept her at home with them, and she went to school in the special-ed program all the way through high school.

It wasn't easy at times, for her parents or for my mom, who was put in charge of keeping watch over her sister, a huge strain on any teenager, let alone one as popular as my mom was. She was made to take Kathy along with her to social events, which caused her to pass on going to some at all. No wonder Jody left home as soon as she could, first living in an apartment nearby while she worked and went to college, then moving to

California when she was twenty-one after a job offer in the music business.

As an adult, standing just under five feet tall, Kathy was shaped a bit like a barrel. She had gray crew-cut hair, bright blue eyes, and her teeth showed even when she closed her mouth, which she rarely ever did. When I was young, her rosy cheeks and button nose reminded me of a Christmas elf. She was kind and loving, and everyone adored her—not just in the family; in the entire community. She remembered the name of anyone she'd ever met. Kathy made you feel as if you were the one most special to her, the kind of person others describe as "my" Kathy.

I adored her most of the time, except for when she tattled on me, which was pretty frequent. She tattled on me for coloring outside the lines in my coloring book. She tattled on me for opening a second can of sardines when I was still hungry after finishing the first. She tattled on me for going into the drawers of my grandma's vanity and putting on her lipsticks. I began doing bad things on purpose just so Kathy would tattle on me. When she realized I was breaking a rule, her eyes would go wide, her nostrils would flare, and her fists would clench as the words came erupting out of her. "Mom, Lucy's doin' somethin' bad!" I would laugh and laugh as she went running to get Wanda.

It was during Kathy's tattling era, when I was about ten, that we were closest. Even though she was in her forties, we seemed the same age to me, and so these memories that I share now are as they would have been with two children.

We had great times together, as we both loved adventure of any kind. I think Kathy's adventurous nature made her like bustling around doing the odd tasks my grandma asked her to help with. Whether it was walking to Schnucks with a thirty-nine-cent coupon to buy a head of iceberg lettuce or getting hot water from the kitchen for my grandma's footbath, Kathy seemed to enjoy the purpose and activity.

In the moments when Kathy could slip away unnoticed, she would tiptoe alllllllll the way over to her bedroom door, which was a scrunching plastic accordion door almost on top of the television set, and sneak into her stash of soda and candy, which she kept hidden under her T-shirts in a drawer. I would watch her do this from the couch. Even though she would seal herself in her bedroom, the scrunching plastic always popped open a bit, so I could see inside. The space between her bed and her dresser was no wider than an airplane aisle, so she could sit on her bed and open the drawer at the same time.

She would take out her huge two-liter soda and, holding it with both hands, chug until she was breathless. Then she would hold the bottle squeezed between her knees and reach back into the drawer for a king-size candy bar. She would take a huge mouthful of chocolate and chew at lightning speed, as if the house was burning down and she couldn't evacuate until she'd finished. The candy was washed down with another long swig of the sugar water, then all the evidence was stuffed hurriedly back into the drawer and covered with the T-shirts. It was a fascinating comedy routine, the best reality show ever, and I was the only one who knew about it.

I would float with Kathy from room to room, pretending to be immersed in my book but recording in my journal what she'd sneak through the house next. She was crafty, checking to her right and left to make sure no one was watching. She never detected me, however. I witnessed Kathy open the fridge daily and shamelessly stick her fingers into any exposed dishes, brazenly swig straight from communal beverages. Mashed potatoes, decimated with finger marks. Grandma's rhubarb pie, devastated by pinches taken. Nothing was safe from Kathy's joyful sampling. Oh, the items would still be served to the family later that day, and needless to say, I had a meager appetite for meals at my grandparents' house. For the record, I never tattled on her.

I REMEMBER THE LAST fishing trip I got to take with Dale, just the two of us, when I was fourteen. I sat next to him in his old clunker of a car as we drove out of town, through cornfields, down dusty dirt roads, to a majestic wooded lake. As always, he did not chitchat, so I took his lead and we drove without a word, apart from the occasional comment when he wanted to show me something along the way. He taught me how to be with someone and not have to fill the air with uncomfortable small talk. Dale never filled space like that.

I rarely find others who can simply be with you in this way. From those childhood moments with my grandfather, I've grown to love silence dearly, to practice it daily as a very necessary part of my sanity. It is only in silence that we can sense our true selves, our ancestors, Creation itself. Every answer is there. Mercy and forgiveness await. Rebirth occurs. Conversely, when we pollute our lives with too much noise, a wealth of brilliance, emotional information, and spiritual support remains lost in the pandemonium of human ego.

Interesting that one of the foundational lessons of my life came from the person I shared the fewest words with. Framed in my house I keep a favorite handwritten poem of his, from a book called *Grandma's Memory Lane: The Poetry of Living,* by June E. Summers. The excerpt is written on a scrap of paper, in his signature cursive I've come to know so well from his letters.

There's a path that leads through the woodland
A path that I love to trod
To get away from this wild world's rush
And be alone with God

Dale carried it in his wallet for years, and that's where my mom found it when he died.

CHAPTER TWO

———

ONLY MINUTES AWAY FROM the nursing home now, and my memories drifted to visiting Dale's mom, my Great-Grandma Ella Marie, there when she was close to one hundred. Her room was only a few doors down from where her daughter-in-law Wanda was now, eighteen years later.

I remember sitting at Marie's feet, I would've been about eight, and thinking how funny her mouth looked with no teeth in it. Her delicate wrinkled lips had depressed where her teeth used to be, and it gave her mouth a permanent pucker. Beautiful and physically bold in youth, she was a frail wisp of a woman, tiny and hunched over, by the time I came along. In my memory, she wore pastel colors. She was the oldest person I had ever seen.

As a kid, I tended to stare unapologetically when I saw someone who fascinated me, and I stared hard at her toothless mouth, wanting desperately to touch her lips and ask her why they looked like that. I was quite intimidated by her, though, so I sat politely and kept my fingers in my lap. I could sense that an enormous expanse of time separated us, as if she and I came from different dimensions, brushing past each other for this brief moment. I felt a reverence for her as one would in the presence of a saint.

One of my earliest memories in life is being in Great-Grandma Marie's tiny cube of a house on Shirley Street, in Newman, before she entered the nursing home. Her husband, my Great-Grandpa Clinton Boyer, had died while in that same nursing home, of Alzheimer's, in 1976. After his death, Marie stayed on at the Boyer farm alone before moving to the Shirley house, where she lived for some years before the nursing home. From my cousins, I've learned that Marie was the epitome of the phrase "Bloom where you are planted," rarely complaining about circumstances in her life, and it was with this optimism in her step that she embraced her move from the farm where she and Clinton had lived for so long.

Who knows how many days I spent there in the town house as a toddler with Marie? If it was more than one, I wouldn't know; they're all melted into one simple memory—one perfect eternal day. To me, her new home was like a dollhouse. Living room, bedroom, bathroom, kitchen, all miniature. It was immaculately clean, with beautiful porcelain knickknacks all around. I remember the curtains drawn against the heat of the sun. In that dark, cool, peaceful world, I was perfectly content.

Out in the heavy sunlight, the house had tall bushes lining it, and a little garden out back past a carport. I remember Marie picking hollyhocks from a tall stalk laden with them and making me dolls, with one flower bud for the head and a blossoming flower for its skirt. She sat me and my flower dolls down at the cold linoleum table in the kitchen and fed us all a delicious lunch of cottage cheese and canned peaches. Funny how children and old people eat the same foods.

25

I've come to learn that Marie was actually an excellent cook in her life, preparing the most delicious homemade food for anyone who dropped by. Her noodles, pies, and signature "homemade mayonnaise" (a creamy pudding with bananas and nuts) were famous with the harvesters, who she always fed, and apparently she could wring a chicken's neck like nobody's business. My mom tells of walking the farm with her Grandma Marie when very young, and Marie saying, "I think we'll have chicken tonight." In the same breath, she would casually stride over to an unassuming chicken, lovingly take it by the neck, and with a few masterful and violent flicks of her wrist, dinner was settled.

Marie made a meal every night, for her visitors, children, and Clinton. Never was a man so beautifully spoiled by his wife; she would lay out all the food and condiments so that he didn't have to reach for anything. Marie didn't eat much herself, too preoccupied with making sure everyone else at the table was taken care of and got enough. I like to think of her with a moment to herself after everyone was fed, enjoying her own meal in peace. God knows I'd want it if I took care of a large family, as Marie did.

Clinton Boyer built their farmhouse for Marie when they married around 1910, on a large farm parcel outside of town. He went all-out to create a beautiful home for his bride, even ordering the doors and windows from the Montgomery Ward catalog, which was very flashy for those parts. It must've been thrilling for Marie, an avid birdwatcher, to enjoy her beloved birds from the dining room as they visited the feeders she hand-mounted on poles and placed in the yard outside her luxury custom windows. Together, she and Clinton created a home, "the Boyer family farm." It became the meeting place for all important family events for the next hundred years, well into my lifetime.

Marie had been a teacher before getting married, and had even dreamed of becoming a doctor. She collected medical journals and kept up with all the latest news in the field. At that time, however, women in her neighborhood didn't become doctors but became pregnant regularly, which she did, with nine children.

Great-Grandpa Clinton was a jack of many trades. In addition to his work as a farmer, he was county treasurer, county assessor, a teacher, even the school principal. After committing himself full-time to farming, he continued to teach Sunday school at the Methodist church near the farm, where the family attended services. He taught because he was literate, which was no small feat in those days.

Clinton was not just literate but an avid lover of poetry, and he liked to read it aloud to anyone who would listen. As his family grew, his children and grandchildren would excitedly climb onto his lap for a poetry reading and, if they were very lucky, a sip of his special cream-and-sugared tea. Growing up, I heard whispers of a darker side to Clinton, kept quiet. Little did I know that Grandma Wanda was about to divulge her own disturbing encounter with this man who had been her father-in-law.

Toward the end of Great-Grandma Marie's life, I wonder how she felt about living alone, and no longer on a farm. She'd spent nearly a century handling turbulent households, endless farming duties, and now...all was silent. Was it finally a relief or was she lonesome? Probably both. Life is always both, isn't it? I wish I could have asked her if she ever longed to see the world—the museums of Europe, the palm trees of a tropical island, live theater in New York City—or was she content right where she was? Perhaps some buried longing for adventure was the reason she had loved her bird watching so much. Maybe she lived vicariously through their freedom.

In my two memories of her, in the dollhouse and sitting at her feet in the nursing home, she is never speaking. I cannot remember her voice at all, much as with her quiet son, my Grandfather Dale. Marie will forever remain with me as silent and gentle—a holy spirit draped in angelic pastel, with a sweet smile but no teeth.

———

I SNAPPED OUT OF my thoughts as I realized that I had entered the township of Newman. I was finally here. Covering only some four hundred acres, Newman had a whopping population of eight hundred fifty-five that January day in 2011. Most of the buildings in town are abandoned, reminders of a bustling past when industry put this place on the map. Even still, Newman boasts an eclectic mix of amenities: one pizza parlor (which I discovered is run by a third cousin I never knew I had until we got to talking), a Dollar General store (of course), an American Legion hall (also of course), a wonderful antique shop, and a café where later, when I ordered a beer, I was told they do not serve beer but would run to the store and buy me one if I wished. *Toto, I have a feeling we're not in L.A. anymore.* I slowed the car as I spotted the Boxwood Nursing Home. *I'm here, Grandma.*

CHAPTER THREE

————

BOXWOOD IS AN L-SHAPED single-story building, with
the windows of residents' rooms lining the front wing.
It sits far back from the road, amidst grassy fields, next
to an eternally empty baseball diamond. It's there for
the surrounding neighborhood, but I never saw a single
game being played during my visits.

Boxwood sits at the very tip of Newman, the last
stop before the farmland stretches out again for miles.
Originally built as an elderly-care facility, it opened
as the Continental Manor in 1974, with my Great-
Grandfather Clinton and other relatives among its first
residents. I parked in a visitor spot, shut the engine off,
and sat for a minute, staring blankly at the brown-brick
facade and burnt-sienna roof. I wondered whose idea
the rather drab color scheme was and decided that if I
ever opened a nursing home, I would make sure it was
painted rainbow.

Come on, let's move. God, I was nervous. I slowed my
breath as I walked up the asphalt drive and through the
automatic double doors.

Every time I had come to visit Grandma Wanda here,
she would be waiting for me just inside the front doors,
on a bench next to the nurses' station. It was her favorite
spot, at the heart of the building, where everyone came
and went. She would warmly greet every person who
passed, whether she knew them or not. With those
who didn't return her salutation, she would call after

them, "It wouldn't hurt you to be friendly!" There was no escaping Wanda Mae's friendship when she set her sights on you.

Today was no exception. I stopped short at the sight of her, sitting there on the wooden bench waiting to receive me, so tiny under the ugly florescent lighting. In this charmless setting, she looked like a flower growing out of concrete, and my heart swelled with tenderness for her. She wore a red knit sweater over a pastel pink turtleneck, pink pants, and white lace-up shoes. Her snow-white hair was teased up into her signature perfectly sheened bubble, and her crooked fingers, folded in her lap, were tipped with red-painted nails. She of course had on full makeup, complete with bright red lipstick; as a rule, she only wore red. She did herself up this way every single day, with total integrity and style.

At ninety-seven, her eyesight was limited to what was right in front of her, so I waited until I got up next to her to say, "Hi, Grandma, it's Lucy, I'm here!"

She threw her hands up in the air and shrieked loud enough to wake the dead. Then she reached out and pulled me close, embracing me with all her might and yelling with joyous excitement, "Luucccyyy, honeeeyyy!" In the same breath, she exclaimed for anyone within earshot, "This is my granddaughter from California, she's here for her school project!" School project? A few nurses gave a polite smile as they hurried on to their many responsibilities.

I was on my knees hugging her and laughing. "I'm here, Grandma, I'm here. You look so beautiful."

She pressed her forehead to mine, our tradition since I was young.

As I stood back so the nurses could transfer her into her wheelchair, my sense of smell finally registered the repulsive mix of pungent urine and putrid sickness, poorly concealed with harsh chemical disinfectant, that permeated every corner of every room. It was not the home's fault, it just comes with getting old. It really upset me for Grandma, though, who always smelled lovely and took great pride in her perfumes. I was so sorry that her own sweet fragrance was now overwhelmed by this highly offensive stench.

Pushing down my disgust, I tried to stay focused on Wanda and not look around. I always trained my eyes on Wanda when visiting, to shut out the sight of old age creeping up over people like parasitic vines overtaking healthy trees. *Don't look, don't look.* But as I wheeled her down the support-bar-lined corridor, my eyes accidentally and inevitably lingered on people along the hallway. The familiar crushing emotions of sadness and concern tightened my chest. I reminded myself that they must also have family who visited. Didn't they? They were not all lost souls, not all. I could convince myself all I wanted, but my pain for them persisted.

As sharp and lively as ever, Wanda was compelled to stop and introduce me to every nurse, every friend, and every stranger along the way.

"This is my granddaughter Lucy from California, she's here for her school project!" she repeated loudly. "Lucy's an actress, she's in the movies." Nobody was impressed, although the orderlies gave gracious performances. Talk about actresses!

A sweet nurse who could've been Dame Judi Dench's twin was rolling a cart with cake and coffee around to the rooms, and when she stopped to meet me, I noticed she made sure to call Wanda by name several times. *So they remember who they are. So they feel human. Bless you, thank you.*

Wanda had known some of her neighbors along this corridor for most of her life, a few of them since kindergarten. Imagine being in a nursing home a lifetime from now with people you knew as a child! So between introductions to these various lifelong familiars, she whispered ancient gossip about them in my ear. Well, not whispered—more like broadcast to anyone within ten feet, because Wanda only ever had one volume: LOUD.

"That's George by the window, he took Meredith's sister to the senior dance, it was scandalous…he's a very bad boy," she whisper-blurted.

"Grandma, he's ninety-eight years old, for God's sake," I whispered uselessly in George's defense.

By the time we made it to her room, number 208, I knew more dusty scandal about the people I had just wheeled past than I know about all of Hollywood put together, and believe me, I know a lot of scandal.

I wheeled Wanda through her door, careful not to hit the frame with her chair, and she wasted no time in proudly giving me the grand tour of her living quarters. Even though the room was cramped, with just one narrow window along the far wall, it was meant to be shared. Boxwood was a roommate establishment, for the most part. The beds were separated by a thin pale pink curtain that offered what privacy could be had, but drawing it was unnecessary at the moment, because Wanda's roommate had died the week before. Grandma had endured more than a few roommates dying, and each time was a distressing loss for her. Studies on the time spent in a nursing home before death vary, but most claim the average stay is thirteen months. Wanda had been here seven years.

I walked to the window, where the cold sun was half-heartedly slanting its rays just a few feet into the room, and pulled the curtains open to reveal frosty grass and naked trees.

"I like it better when the trees and flowers bloom out there," Wanda said. "I can watch 'em all swayin' in the breeze. I always love that." A life where the day's entertainment was watching the flowers and trees sway—so foreign to my city life of cement and traffic. It sounded lovely and thrilling and deeply peaceful, and I suddenly yearned for it right along with Wanda.

As I set my things on the empty bed, she asked me to bring out a shoebox from her closet, and opened it to show me her beloved collection of greeting cards. Wanda saved practically every single card she had ever received. She also loved sending them: Through the years, I've gotten many sappy Hallmark cards from her, some with a crisp new five-dollar bill within. Since she's not a woman of many written words, they are for the most part simply signed, "I love you so much, Grandma." Her handwriting was always scraggly, barely legible, as if she were writing with her non-dominant hand for a joke. It reminded me that her schooling had ended when she dropped out of high school midway through for personal reasons, as I was about to learn about in more depth.

Grandma showed me her portable-radio headset, which she said she used every night to take the edge off her deep loneliness in the wee hours, when it was the worst. How she stuck it on her head without ruining her expertly bubbled hair, I don't know. Next was her collection of cherished stuffed-animal cats. There were about a dozen of them, all lined up on her bed. She went down the line and introduced me to each one, in its own unique voice and attitude that she had invented. Her favorite of the litter was an orange-and-white-striped cat my mom had given to her. She slept with him every night.

The destitute mind, no matter its age, creates unusual connections for survival and sanity; think of Wilson, the volleyball in Tom Hanks's film *Castaway*. Or your own childhood comfort object, which you needed with you at all times or life would fall apart. Yet another parallel between children and old people. For me, it was a blankie…well, not a blankie but a *song about* a blankie that I clung to. The song *about* the blankie *was* my blankie. I had to listen and sing along to that musical story on cassette tape every single day, or else.

Don't wash my blanket, don't take it away
I want to drag it around while I play
To me it's okay dirty and gray

Please don't wash my blanket today
I might get lonely, I might get scared
I need to know that my blanket is there, so....

These stuffed-animal cats were some of Wanda's most important comforts now, and so I humored her and met them all down the line.

When we had quite finished with the cats, Wanda showed me her proudest possession: her battery-powered, forty-nine-key Yamaha electronic keyboard. The PSR-6 model featured one hundred preset voices (not one of which sounded remotely good), ten rhythms, and real-time melody memory. It was the centerpiece of the room, and just as she'd draped her living room armchair with doilies, she kept a beautifully crocheted cream-colored cover over it when she wasn't playing. Her fingers were so crooked they looked like spindly twigs, but she joyfully played her keyboard and sang every day. In fact, in the nursing home she had been given her own music hour, "Wanda's Melodies," every Tuesday for all to enjoy.

She wheeled her chair up to the keyboard. There was always a song on the tip of her tongue, and today it was "Church in the Wildwood." There's "no lovelier spot in the dale...as the little brown church in the vale." As with most standard items in Wanda's life, she spiced things up with her own twist, and I quite preferred her version:

Come come come to the church in the wildwood,
Oh, come to the church in the dell
No spot is so dear to my childhood

36

As the little brown church in the dell
In the dell
In the dell

On the final stop of our bedroom tour, I was asked to bring a second shoebox from the closet. This time it was her "surprise box," in which she kept a horde of snacks for her visitors: candy bars, Fig Newtons, peanuts, and those neon-orange-cracker sandwiches with processed peanut butter, which we all recognize but nobody actually knows what they're called. Wanda insisted I take a snack to put in my purse for later, and even though I knew I wouldn't eat any of it, I thanked her and chose the mystery-orange peanut butter crackers.

I've heard that people who've lived through a war share common habits like hiding money in books and keeping food stashed away like this. I knew both were true of her. Wanda had lived through not one but both world wars. She kept her food, her money, her faith, and her loved ones close.

All the while she was showing me her things and giving me the tour, I had been scoping out the room for the best spot in which to film our talk. I was thinking with both sides of my brain, the half that was enjoying spending time with her and the half with a job to do and a tight timeframe in which to do it. I decided to sit her in the middle of the room, facing her bed, with the feeble sunlight from the window streaming in on her right.

As I wheeled her to the spot, I noticed for the first time an obnoxiously loud alarm clanging out in the hall. It would continue incessantly, every few minutes, for my entire three-day visit. Wanda had mentioned that she was enraged by it, pushed to her wits' end by having to endure it twenty-four hours a day. I agreed, it was enough to make anyone lose their mind. We both ignored it as best we could.

As I set up my filming equipment as nonchalantly as possible, I explained that we would simply be chatting, as she had wanted, and that I would be filming her, but she didn't have to worry about anything. I was hurrying, because I could see she was eyeing my camera and movements suspiciously, and I didn't want to give her time to shrink away from our talk.

She studied me with her hands folded in her lap. "I thought you was gonna interview some of the other folks in the nursin' home, too?"

I kept my voice as casual as I could. "Nope, I just want to talk to you."

Her brow was becoming furrowed with confusion. "Oh, I didn't get it that way at all, I didn't get it that way, not at all…. I thought you was gonna bring a whole bunch of cameras an' talk to the others here for your schoolwork."

I sugarcoated my words as I fumbled to focus the camera on her face. "Grandma, I haven't been in school for years. I started touring with my music right after high school, remember?"

"Oh, sure," she murmured with a frown. I wondered how she had swung from not wanting any cameras on her to expecting multi-cams. "Well, you're gonna break all your cameras if it's just me you're filmin', hon."

I briskly moved to my chair, next to the camera,

before she had a chance to backtrack any further.

"Let's talk now, shall we?"

She nodded and waited, holding her breath. I held mine, too.

Here we go. I pressed Record.

CHAPTER FOUR

Lucy: What is your name?
Wanda: I can't hear ya, hon.

I leaned forward in my chair and raised my voice considerably.

Lucy: What is your name?
Wanda: Wanda.
Lucy: What is your full name?
Wanda: Wanda Mae Boyer.
Lucy: When were you born?
Wanda: On August 16, 1913.
Lucy: And where were you born?
Wanda: In North Mayview, Illinois…on a farm.

When Wanda was born, the village of Mayview was thriving, with a one-room schoolhouse, a green-roofed church, and several businesses, although, since it is no more than an unincorporated township, no past population census exists. Scarcely twenty dwellings remain today.

Lucy: Can you tell me about the house you were born in?
Wanda: We lived in a beautiful two-story old wooden-framed house. An' it had five rooms downstairs an' three bedrooms upstairs. An' it was a nice big ol' farm home, I loved it dearly an' so did my mom an' dad. My dad run a three-hundred-fifty-acre farm, an' we just

got along real good out there in the country. The house was a very, very sacred thing. It's been torn down an' a new one put up in its place now. But we still cherish the thoughts of the old house, because it was a really beautiful place.

We had a dinin' room, sittin' room, parlor...what they called a parlor in those days...an' a livin' room. An' we had a piano in there, an' my mom played by ear, the same as I do, the same as you do. She played piano an' sang beautiful, sang beautiful. An' my dad just knew a coupla songs, but he managed to get along an' be a good farmer...he was a good farmer.

Lucy: Did your dad build the house?

Wanda: Oh, no, uh-uh, no. It was built before we bought it...I don't know who built it, unless Grandpa Thompson might've had a hand in it. He was my mom's dad...Thompson was her maiden name.

Lucy: What was your mother's married name?

Wanda: Nellie Mae Roughton.

Lucy: And what was your father's name?

Wanda: Frank Ulmont Roughton.

Lucy: Tell me about your mother's personality.

Wanda: My mother's personality was out of this world. The most lovin', kind-hearted, good woman. An' she had such a big family that she just went right along with us an' everythin' we partook in, an' everythin' went along real good. An' she was one heck of a good cook; she could just look at a pie an' make it. She was the most wonderful cook you ever seen... she could make homemade noodles that would melt in your mouth. Every day she done somethin' that made me love her an' love her some more.

Lucy: Where were your parents born?

Wanda: My dad was born in these parts, but his dad was English; all of his relations was born an' raised in England. An' Mom was born in Hannibal, Missouri… right here in the United States. But they got together some way or another, an' married, an' then she always took care of the family, an' he done the farmin' an' the heavy work. She done plenty of it, too, washin' clothes on a board.

Lucy: That's how you did laundry.

Wanda: Oh, yeah, that's the only way we could.

Lucy: What chores did you do when you were young?

Wanda: Well, milk the cows…an' I took care of the chickens by the dozens, an' I had somethin' to do all the time. There wasn't never a dull moment, except to go to bed an' get some shuteye an' some rest, because you was just so busy from one thing into another. It was very, very good-like, so good on my mother's part an' my father's, too.

Lucy: There were twelve children?

Wanda: Yes, but the first one was stillborn…the boy, an' then the rest were all livin'. My sisters were Violet, Kate, Grace, Guyneth, Ethel, an' my brothers were Paul Edward, Kenneth Enoch, Harold, Frankie, an' Howard. An' everybody's gone now but me, I'm the only one still livin' out of the whole big family.

Lucy: Who was your favorite sibling?

Wanda: My favorite brother was Howard, just younger than me in the boys. An' then the girls, I think mostly Guynie. Guyneth was her real name, Guyneth Minerva Roughton. An' let's see, Violet, the oldest girl. They was my favorite sisters. But they're all gone now.

Lucy: Are you the youngest?

Wanda: I'm the youngest girl. I had three younger brothers, they all died a long while back, a long while. Howard died of a stroke at sixty-six. Paul died of a… well, he had complications. An' so he lived to be only, oh, sixty-somethin'. Then little Harold was hurt at school, a swing hit him on the back of the mastoid bone, in the back of yer ear. He was eight an' a half when he died with the shattered bone behind his neck.

Lucy: Can you tell me about what happened?

Wanda: He was at the country school in the lunch hour, an' he came around the swings, an' a boy was swingin' up in the air, an' he swang right into Harold's head. Harold thought the boy was kiddin' him about a girlfriend, an' Harold said, "I never did that!!"…an' he forgot where he was, an' run right under the swing. An' of course the swings in those days—the board was wide an' thick, an' they had steel pieces holdin' 'em on the chains that swung 'em. An' he just run underneath the boy swingin' up, an' it cost him his life. He died about a week later.

Lucy: Tell me about Harold's singing.

Wanda: Harold was the most beautiful singer. He went to his deathbed singin' "Tiptoe Through the Tulips" …an' he just sang an' sang an' sang. He was the darlingest little boy you ever seen, a nice-lookin' little boy. Him an' I just was as close together as a sister an' brother could ever be, an' it was the most wonderful,

wonderful thing. We had the best life together with each other. I loved him dearly an' he loved me dearly. We had a lot in common with our singin' an' music.

Wanda was eighteen years old when her youngest brother was hit by the swing in 1931. The two shared a bed in the attic, and although ten years apart in age, they were indeed the best of friends. Harold and Wanda made the most of having to share cramped quarters, laughing and singing harmonies deep into the long nights. Knowing Wanda, she would've woven stories for her brother from stardust and moonbeams, while he absorbed every word like precious treasure.

Harold was wounded on the playground on April 2, an ordinary school day. The impact of the blow left him unconscious on the dirt, with seemingly only a badly bleeding gash behind his ear. As awestruck children gaped and confused adults came running, he regained consciousness and was driven home by his teacher. He appeared to be shaken and quiet but alert. Little could they have known at the time that his skull was badly fractured, and his brain was already beginning to swell.

The family physician, Doctor D.E. Yantis, was summoned and, immediately alarmed by Harold's disoriented state, ordered he be taken to nearby Burnham Hospital. As delirious hours turned into several days and Harold hung onto life, it seemed he might actually recover. He was, after all, conscious and, the story goes, even singing! That would give anybody cause to hope. But brain injuries can be deceiving, and as the swelling continued for a whole week, Harold took a whole bunch of bad turns and slipped toward death. He died at five-fifty p.m. on April 10, eight days after he was hurt.

As unbelievable as it sounds that he could've been singing up until the end, it's true. Even the newspaper articles of the day confirmed it. I have snippets of three original articles from the tragedy, which all tell of this extraordinary little boy singing what they called "Tripping Thru the Tulips" as he died. One of the articles says, "He made a brave fight for life but lost. He had a love for music and at the hospital often sang and asked that his sisters sing with him. He sang just a short time before he passed away."

A second reads, "Harold was the youngest of eleven children. For eight and one half years he was permitted to be the sunshine of the home into which he was born. He was much loved by his little friends at school, and up to the very last he welcomed their visits. All through his illness, he bore up like a little soldier. He constantly expressed himself in song that comforted his family and furnished an outlet for his own brave little spirit. His favorite song—the last one he sung—was 'Tripping Thru the Tulips.'"

Out with a song, what a way to go. It occurs to me as I write this that Harold might have been singing because he was scared. I say that because I sing to self-soothe in moments of distress, and I've heard of others doing so. Maybe Harold, too? Who knows.

The third article is strictly factual. To determine whether the nature of Harold's death was suspicious, Coroner William Strode held an inquest hearing at the funeral home the morning after Harold's death, at which his father and Dr. Yantis testified. A small jury was formed, and their verdict was "We the jury, find that Harold Ervin Roughton came to his death from a fracture of the skull resulting from an injury he received at the Northview school playground, April 2, 1931. We are of the opinion that the incident was purely accidental in nature."

Harold's funeral was held just two days after he died. He was buried at Mount Olive Cemetery, beside two plots that would be his parents' when their times came. Almost my entire family has joined Harold and his parents in that cemetery, and so I have visited often. Whenever I do, I sit beside little Harold's grave. I sing to him. It's peaceful there, nestled among the cornfields. The grass whispers in the wind as if sharing secrets with the departed, birds fuss in the brush, trucks pass on the highway; the rhythms of life persist, unaware of the past or future. Whether the sky is high and bright with sun or low and heavy with rain, its restlessness is a constant reminder of the onward flow of time—that generations have passed since that little boy lived.

I was fortunate to end up with one of the only existing photographs of Harold; I keep it with Wanda's photograph on a special shelf in my house. As with Dale's letters, I think heirlooms find their way to the right people, and joyful, musical, eternal Harold is safe with me.

CHAPTER FIVE

Lucy: Do you remember falling out of the second-story window when you were a toddler?

Wanda: Oh, my gosh, we had a two-story house, so the three bedrooms was upstairs. Mom had said to my two oldest sisters, Grace an' Violet, "You girls get yer broom an' mop, an' clean the upstairs rooms." So they decided to take me along, an' we went upstairs to the west room. The windows in every room upstairs was only about a foot from the floor, an' they opened the window clear up to the sash.

I was just learnin' to walk, a little over a year old—an' I went over, sat down in the window, an' fell clear out backwards, sixteen foot down to the ground. Fell right on my face an' my stomach, knocked every bit of wind an' air out of my stomach. My uncle is the one who picked me up, my mom's brother, an' they had the doctor out, an' he said, "She's lucky she's alive"… as young as I was when I fell. But it just worked out that way.

Mom was bathin' me an' cleanin' me up later, an' she discovered my nose was broken. An' that's what it did, broke my nose. Therefore, I've always had quite of a bump there, always have…until not too long ago, I fell right here at the nursin' home, an' it unbroke. The nurse said, "You're going to be tickled to death, Wanda, you don't have that bump on your nose anymore." I said, "Oh, I am absolutely thrilled to death." So, it all turned out real good, as good as could be expected.

We had a good laugh over this before we gathered ourselves again. What a fantastic perspective Wanda had on life...to feel that her broken nose had worked out positively, ninety-five years later. She was a very tough woman but brimming with optimism—running through her veins, coming out her ears. I learned from my grandmother that optimism is the ultimate life hack. It was her superpower. When life gave Wanda lemons, she not only made lemonade, she invited the whole neighborhood to her lemonade-stand party and shared it, on the house.

Lucy: Who were your best friends growing up?

Wanda: Actually, I just kind of meandered with all of 'em. I didn't have no actual girlfriends—you mean young schoolmates? No, I didn't, I just loved 'em all an' that was about it. My country school was real good, they taught an' taught real, real good.

Lucy: Who was your favorite teacher?

Wanda: My favorite teacher was the first one I had, an' the second one. Their names was Miss O'Toole, she never was married, an' the next one was Mrs. Whistiff. Mrs. Whistiff got married when she was teachin' me. They were good, learnable teachers. I mean, they were gooooood.

Lucy: Did you ever get in bad trouble in school?

Wanda: I was chewin' some gum, an' you wasn't supposed to do that at all. So the teacher said, "Wanda, what have you got in your mouth?" I said, "Some chewin' gum." Here she come, in a dead race practically, an' she slapped me a blow. It rung up in that schoolroom an' all the kids laughed. An' she turned around to them, an' she said, "Listen, I didn't discipline that girl to have you all laugh at what I did to her. She knew she wasn't supposed to chew gum." That was about my worst discipline.

Lucy: When you were little, what did you think you wanted to pursue when you got older?

Wanda: I didn't have anythin' too much in mind. I married the first time when I was just eighteen, an' was just expected to be married.

Lucy: You've been married twice; how did you meet your first husband?

Wanda: His name was Henry Ervin Sadler. Sadler was my first last name, after I married him. He kinda knew my family, an' he kept comin' around an' makin' excuses that he was comin' to visit my mom an' dad, an' all the time he was comin' to see me. An' therefore, we got married, had two boys.

I knew going deeper into what she had just said would expose a nerve, so I spoke gently.

Lucy: Tell me about your first baby.

Wanda: My first baby died, he died at two an' a half months old. His name was Donald Lee Sadler. He had been born with the openin' of his stomach grown shut. We had him operated on, but he died about a half a hour after they operated. Then about three years later, I had Henry Ervin II, an' he's still livin' in California, as you well know.

I do know. My Uncle Burb and Aunt Sis, as they're nicknamed, live an hour from me in Los Angeles. Although I rarely see them, in my younger days I got to visit them every few months with my mom, Jim Dad, Grace, and Spencer. My Uncle Burb has always been ridiculously handsome, with the looks and cool of Paul Newman, and hilariously funny to boot. He has the same wickedly playful sense of humor as his mama, that infectious Roughton joy. Our games included him tweaking my nose or threatening to tickle me if I got too close, sending me into fits of laughter as I'd run away. I loved our time together. Aunt Sis is more serious than Burb but just as loving. They've been together since high school.

Their home is really intriguing, a one-story lodge-like abode of dark wood, with hunting rifles and taxi-dermied birds on the walls. Antique furniture from their Illinois country beginnings fills each room, including a massive player piano in the living room that cranked charmingly out-of-tune ragtime hits. I loved to gather my family and "give concerts," pretending it was me playing. Their house smelled like menthol tobacco, leather, history—I swear history has a smell.

Our visits were mostly spent in front of the TV, where Uncle Burb was glued to his Nascar races. During a visit in 2001, watching the live broadcast of the Daytona 500 together, we witnessed the death of racer Dale Earnhart, Sr., when he crashed his stock car on the final turn of the final lap. How devastating for his family to see it happen in front of them.

Also devastating to think about what my grandmother had just said, that she lost her first child, who would've been my Uncle Henry's older brother, when she was nineteen years old. What baby Donald died of was *achalasia*, a neuromuscular disorder of the esophagus. In brief, the muscles fail to propel food into the stomach, the food comes back up, and the victim can starve, choke to death, or develop pneumonia. It tends to be very rare in infants. Achalasia became considerably more curable in the nineteen fifties, two decades after Wanda lost her newborn to it in 1932—just a year after she lost her brother to the swing accident.

The woman had gone through some hellish trauma before she was twenty. These heart-wrenching setbacks must have severely disrupted her sense of security and trust in the world. Anyone who endures extreme loss can attest that it is the stealer of hope, of a feeling of possibility. I think it made her involuntarily toughen up to get through it and never dare dream of anything more than what was given, lest it be taken away as well. It was this mix of toughness and gratitude for what she had that drove her personality to the end.

Lucy: How did you feel the first time you got pregnant?

Wanda: I didn't think too much about it. In those days, you had children just like clockwork, or my mom woulda never had twelve children. That's the way it was, you had no preventatives. You had nothin' but just yourself to add to it. So therefore, you had to take what the good Lord see'd fit to give you. That's what my mom did, an' that's what I did. I had five children—

two boys by my first marriage an' three girls by Dale Boyer, your mom Jody bein' the youngest.

Lucy: When was the first time you fell in love?

Wanda: Well, that was a very long time ago, when we was still livin' in the house where I was born in Mayview. I fell in love with Henry Sadler. I loved both of my husbands. Just because I divorced the first one didn't mean I didn't love him, because I did. But he was always lookin' at other women an' doin' things to, uh, oh, keep me upset most of the time. He was kinda cruel, we'll put it that way. He drank an awful lot, an' I had to get away from him, because he tried to kill me a couple times. I just had to get away from him before he killed me, so I divorced him.

Lucy: Why did he try to kill you?

Wanda: Well, because of his drinkin'. It got through his nerves, an' through his whole system. He was just made that way, just made that way. Just mean, just mean. After a few drinks, they took hold an' he was real…real…bad, real bad. Of course, I was not innocent, don't get me wrong, but I wasn't ornery, I was not ornery.

This was all referring to an incident in the newlyweds' kitchen that she would go on to tell me more about in the coming days. Henry, in an impassioned rage, had gone after Wanda with a broken alcohol bottle. There was shattered glass, blood, screaming. The police were called, and Henry was arrested.

He was the definition of a bad boy, and Wanda had felt the timeless fascination for this archetype that so many of us women share. I already knew quite well that she had dropped out of high school and married Henry Sadler in large part to escape the abuse she had endured at home from her own alcoholic father. It is textbook that she would've confused Henry's rough physical attention for love, since she had known a lifetime of it. She had run straight from one abuser into the arms of another.

Lucy: Tell me about you…didn't they call your family the Rotten Roughtons?

Wanda: Oh, yeah, always did. The Rotten Roughtons. Roughton was our maiden name. But we was good people, good people. We was just always findin' ourselves in the middle of trouble of all sorts.

Lucy: Why did they call you that?

Wanda: Well, because we always had an answer for everythin', an' always had a joke to tell. Our mama was a real cut-up. So consequently, we kids come along an' most of us was quite a bit like Mama, which I was very thankful for, 'cause my dad was set in his ways, an' stubborn as a mule.

Lucy: Was your family religious?

Wanda: Well, my mother was quite a bit, but my father wasn't too much. We went to the Mayview church. I loved church, an' so did Mom. An' we put on a show once a year around Christmastime at home, all of us joined in, we was always actin' people. We had an attic, what we called a *scuddy*, in our big home out in the country.

The definition of *scuddy* in urban-slang dictionaries

refers to something like a low-class/white-trash person, and in Scotland, "in the skud" means *naked*. I have no idea why Wanda's family used it to describe their attic— although both those definitions are definitely in line with their family nickname and reputation at the time.

Wanda: It was a long room, an' we'd hang up a wire an' we'd put a blanket over that wire, an' that would be the window...the thing for the show to start...you know, ah, uh...I'm tryin' to say...uh....

Lucy: A curtain?

Wanda: A curtain, yeah, that's what I'm tryin' to say. We would all get up there an' perform some kind of singin' or dancin', or just most anythin' we could think up. Then we'd just pull the curtain closed when we was through. It was a little showplace is what it was. Our family was always the "show kind." Show, show, show everythin' you done. We was all made that way, just that vibration. Just loved singin' an' playin' an' doin' everythin', we always did. We'd have a regular ball when we'd get together in that show room...just have a regular showdown.

Lucy: Did you want to become an actress when you grew up?

Wanda: Somewhat...I loved movies. We'd go to town, up to the Princess Theater in Urbana, an' see a movie every weekend. My mom loved westerns. I didn't care for 'em too much, I liked the more up an' comin' an' goin' ones. That little theater showed a western every Saturday. So there was Mom, in a whole ring of children, a whole sidewalk covered with 'em—an' her right in the middle, the only old woman…well, she wasn't even old at that time. An' boy, I tell you, she'd get inside an' see that movie, she loved every part of it. An' when they'd shoot off all them guns, gossssshhh! An' fight with one another constantly! She'd just get the biggest kick out of that. She looked forward to her movies on Saturday, always did, always, always did. I don't think my dad went to three movies altogether in his life, I don't think he ever did. But my mom made up for it.

Lucy: Tell me about your favorite holidays with your family.

Wanda: Well, I think my favorite holidays was Thanksgivin' an' Christmas. Mom made a huge meal for Thanksgivin', with everythin' to go with it. Two different kinds of pie, and everythin' else that you could imagine. She was the greatest cook. An' my dad loved his food, so naturally she cooked everythin' for him, there wasn't no foolishness about that.

An' boy, I tell ya, Christmastime, I remember the last Christmas I had at home. My brother Frankie, his birthday was the fifteenth of August, an' mine was the sixteenth, but I would say he was about twenty years older than me…boy, he was somethin'…. Frankie played Santa Claus, dressed all up in as much make-believe as Santa Claus was supposed to wear. He come in the west door—that door was never used, only for real good company, or somethin' of that sort. But he come in that door ringin' some little bells, an' there was us little kids, all draped around on the floor, sittin' on our hands an' knees, ya know, an' boy…. I said, "Wait, that looks just like my brother Frankie's shoes!" an' I was pointin' right at his feet, an' it was him! Later we got such a kick out of that, but at the time, we actually didn't know it was our brother, we actually didn't know.

Lucy: Did you get gifts at Christmas?

Wanda: I think I had three dolls with artificial hair, but I don't think we…well, Dad an' Mom didn't go out an' spend a lot of money, because we just had too many family members to keep, an' too much to do for it. So they didn't do a whole lot of spending on gifts.

Lucy: What about clothes?

Wanda: Mom made all of ours, an' with all us kids it was all hand-me-downs an' things of that sort. Mom was a great sewer, she could sew anythin', even cut them patterns out an' everythin', even cut them patterns out. I don't know how she did it, but she did. An' she papered the walls…she papered every room in that big house, an' those rooms had nine-foot ceilin's! She'd get her paintin' board up, an' then she'd say, "You children have got to stay away from that board, because I keep my pastes on it for pasting my wallpaper."

So we moseyed around the board, kinda teasin' her that we was gonna touch it. All of a sudden, first thing you know, I'd be pastin' the paper for Mom to paper the rooms. She could make every pattern fit together… if it was flowered, the flowers went right together. An' when she got through with a room, you could've thought that a regular paperhanger had been there! But that was her talent, she could do anythin'. Anythin' there was to do, she could do it.

Lucy: How was your relationship with your father?

Wanda: That relationship went as far as, uh…not

good. My dad was a heavy whiskey drinker, an' Mom didn't drink at all. Dad needed his socializin' an' Mom usually drove him, since he would drink. He would go into town an' play Euchre [a "trick-taking" card game that became popular in the U.S. in the mid–eighteen hundreds] with the fellas, an' Mom would sit in the car an' wait for him to finish. Their relationship with each other was performed mostly at night, mostly. That's why we had such a big family. But she never allowed him to bring his whiskey home, he always bought whiskey in them little half-pint bottles an' finished 'em away from the home.

Lucy: How did his drinking make you feel?

Wanda: Well, it didn't set well with none of us. Some of his kids turned out to be beer drinkers, but never whiskey drinkers, but he was. He swilled on that whiskey, 'cause he loved it, he loved the taste of it. I couldn't even smell it, 'cause it was just…ewww, horrible, I didn't like it at all. But I had to learn to like beer, because Dale loved his beer, he loved his beer.

Lucy: So you were closer with your mother than your father?

Wanda: I was close to my mother, as close as anythin' you ever seen in your life. Always was, always was. Closest little soul.

Lucy: Was moving away from home a happy thing, or did something happen that made you move?

Wanda: Well, I got married pretty young the first time, and that's why I left. I think I wanted to get away from the drinkin', but I went straight to another drinker somehow.

Lucy: Where was your first wedding?

Wanda: Olney, Illinois. One of my sisters was married in Olney, an' her husband talked my husband an' I into goin' down there an' gettin' married.

Lucy: Grandma, I want to go back to Harold for a minute. How did your family cope after your brother Harold died?

Wanda: Well, Mom couldn't hardly cope with it at all, because she was so attached to Harold. An' I was so attached to him, too. So between her an' I, we talked a lot about him, what him an' I used to do together. Day by day, my mother never forgot. She grieved over my brother 'til her dyin' day.

My mom always said, "When I go completely blind, I want to die." An' that's what she did. Her eyes ended up sunk in her head about an inch farther than what they was supposed to be. Her brother was that way an' her sister, too. An' that's the way I feel about my eyesight, too. It's so bad now, and I'm quite a bit like my mom. So therefore I also say, "When I go totally blind, I want the good Lord to take me, too...because it's time for me to move on, it's time."

See, I'm ninety-seven an' I've had a full life, a full life—two husbands, five children, five grandchildren, two great-grandchildren. An' you think back over your life, an' you think, "How much more can you be thankful for that you haven't gave God thanks for already? How much more can you do?"

But I still remember the pain of Harold, an' that's why I keep myself busy here at the home. I fix the bathroom, I clean up stuff just throwed around, I do everythin' I can think up. I paddle back and forth with my old broken-down knees. I do different things just like my mom did to keep herself busy, an' now I see why she kept so busy towards the end, same as me…it was partly because she never got over Harold's death, she never got over it. We've gone crazy thinkin' on it for so very long. You understand why…her lovin' heart said, "No, I'll never forget that boy, I'll never forget him. He's in my heart, and he's gonna stay there."

She was the best little woman, the best. I loved her dearly, an' she loved me dearly, an' she loved all my children wholeheartedly. She knew that life is too short to heckle over. So worship the ground your loved ones walk on, hon, because it's a long road without them. My mom outlived my dad, same as I've outlived my husband. My dad was sixty-nine an' my mom was seventy-seven years old when they each passed away.

Lucy: I think your mom's memory gives you a lot of strength.

Wanda: Oh, yeah, she was just the ideal person. My dad, however, was mean, he was mean when he drank. Not on her, but to us kids, you know, he would just take his spite out on us. She didn't like that part, boy, she hated that.

Lucy: How would he take his spite out on the kids?

Wanda: He'd slap us a dirty one or harm us some way or another. He'd meet us at the entrance to the driveway, an' he had a switch off of a tree without any leaves on it whatsoever, an' he'd smack our legs, our bare legs. We didn't wear stockin's until we was great big kids, so he could just spank our bare legs with them switches...boy, it was horrible. But then the very next day he'd sober up, an' forgot about it, just like that, forgot about it.

Lucy: Are you still angry about things he did to you, even though he's gone?

Wanda: Yeah. We had a horrible, horrible, very slow life. But it paid off.

That comment caught me off guard. Had I heard her right?

Lucy: Why do you say you had a horrible, slow life?

Wanda: Oh, well, we had a good life overall, but it was rough at times, hon. All lives are pretty rough, but they are what you make of 'em, that's what you do. We had a very decent life, but it was rough, it was very rough. Yes, we was called Rotten Roughtons, an' more or less most of us lived right up to the name. My brother Kenneth, he was somethin'.

Lucy: Was Kenneth the worst?

Wanda: He was the oldest boy, and he was a drinker, just drank like a fish. Liquor causes an awful lot of trouble in the long run, which it did with our family.

Lucy: Do you think a lot of our family members have been alcoholics?

Wanda: Well, not so much alcoholics, just, uh.....

As Grandma was struggling to come up with some justification of the alcoholism that indeed plagued her family, one of the nurses stuck her head in and told us that lunch was about to be served in the dining room.

CHAPTER SIX

THAT DAMN ALARM IN the hall was still sounding, and the corridors were bustling with activity as residents were wheeled and led into the dining room. I wheeled Wanda down the corridor alongside everyone else.

Many residents spent their entire day in that dining hall, which doubled as the day room. It was lined with windows that faced the baseball diamond and the road. It was such a nice concept to be able to watch games on that field, except that, as I've said, I never saw any being played. I wished in that moment I could find some volunteer ballplayers so the residents could watch a baseball game with their lunch. Add it to my mental list of what I'd provide my rainbow-painted nursing homes of the future. Ball games for the soul.

In the dining hall, people dotted the linoleum floor in their wheelchairs and faded, sagging recliners. The piercing sound of deep, hacking coughs was constant. The television was permanently on, tuned to daytime soaps. As I wheeled Wanda past the TV set, she loudly told three half-awake men that watching the television that close would rot their brains if they sat there all day. This was a funny comment coming from her, because I have such childhood memories of her sitting two feet away from her TV for hours, watching *The Price Is Right* or *Jeopardy*, sometimes placing a huge magnifying lens in front of the screen to enlarge the flashing images. These three men, however (and most of the residents placed in front of the set), were barely even watching. Some hung their heads; one man appeared to be sleeping, though his eyes were open.

While Wanda did love her TV in earlier decades, this place had made her despise it. She would often urge her neighbors to turn off the set—to converse, play games, or sing instead. She complained that she didn't have any friends in the home, and I could see why. Most had given up on socializing, while she had not. She was an antsy outcast among those biding their time. It angered her, made her cuss and spit fire.

People sitting like lumps where they were placed was a disturbing sight, I had to admit. As I passed a table of four slumped-over humans, heads on their chests, I thought of the terrifying bottom line: that one day this could be me, seemingly forgotten somewhere on the edge of town, staring at the floor. It could be any of us.

Of course, I pretended I was fine. What else could I do? I felt like screaming, "THIS IS TOO HEAVY FOR ME TO HANDLE. I WANT TO FIX IT SOMEHOW FOR YOU ALL BUT I CAN'T, AND THAT'S INFURIATING AND DEVASTATING AND DEEPLY PSYCHOLOGICALLY DISTURBING!"

Nooooo, I couldn't say any of that. Respectfully, it was these people's lives, not mine, and I couldn't save everyone, a confusing concept I've grappled with my entire life. Wanda grappled with it, too, apparently.

As we wheeled over to her table, I offered a bright smile to anyone who would look up, but I made sure to keep my eyes moving over their faces, careful not to look at anyone too long. I wished there were an instruction book on social etiquette in this situation. Where was the line between appropriate salutation and intrusion? Do you try to converse or let them be? To witness these lovely people all up in their personal space as they lost control of their bodies and minds felt like a violation of their privacy, and yet their privacy no longer existed.

I know if it were me, I wouldn't want to be bothered at all hours of the day by passing strangers, just because that stranger felt it was polite...but I also wouldn't mind a little human connection now and then. I'm telling you, the debate within myself has been a lifelong perplexity.

When we finally reached Wanda's table, I nervously chatted with the nurses, overcompensating to lift the mood and breathe life into the atmosphere. There were four people to each square table, and at Wanda's was a lady named Millie and two gentlemen, Bill and George—the same George we had wheeled passed earlier as Wanda whisper-yelled his dirty laundry in my ear. I pulled a spare chair up between Grandma and Millie and created a place setting for myself on the corner of the table, even though I wasn't sure I'd actually be eating whatever the meal was.

Grandma immediately went to work fussing with the placement of her silverware, and then with every-one else's. She told Bill to put his napkin in his lap, she shifted the salt and pepper shakers, she fluffed the fake red and white carnations in their centerpiece vase. She was clearly the social director at her table. No one complained; they all seemed to know and accept the drill. The dynamics among the four seemed the same

63

as with toddlers: one authoritative and opinionated, one annoyed, another appeasing, the other withdrawn. The parallels of old versus young just kept coming, easier to see in this controlled setting than out in the world, where we can hide our vulnerabilities behind our independent actions.

Not long into Wanda's revamping, the meal was served in plastic trays, the kind that are divided into compartments. To start was an appetizer of pineapple rings and cottage cheese. The main course was a very thin piece of pork with an applesauce topping on a mound of room-temperature creamed spinach. In the smallest compartment sat a bite-size chocolate cake in chocolate syrup.

The sunlight in the room was bright, as if a cloud had lifted, and as the food was now fully distributed, the noises of eating were all around. I was presented with my own tray, and at my corner of the table, I ate minuscule bites from each compartment as I pushed the food around to appear to be eating.

It caught my attention that the expected background buzz of conversation was missing. Nobody spoke except for Grandma, who continued to fret with her neighbors' eating habits throughout the meal. It may not have been her place to tell George to sit up or Millie to stop eating with her hands, but I got it: Wanda insisted that those around her conduct themselves as citizens of the world and participate in their lives, while they were still alive. She was striving for order and dignity, when those things were falling apart around her.

As the silent lunch was winding down, Grandma

turned to me. "Hon, go to the piano an' play everyone a song, for their digestion."

Some were already being wheeled back to the television set, which had continued its low drone all through lunch. Several ladies looked eager to watch the soap opera just starting, so I said, "Grandma, I don't think I should play right now; they want to watch their program."

"No, they don't," she insisted. "They don't know what they want." She was assertive, that's for sure. I loved her for it, but not in that moment.

The piano was in the far corner near the TV, and I slowly tiptoed over, reluctantly sat on the worn bench, and began to play a song I had written a few years earlier. I swear I heard a muffled "Shut up" wafting from somewhere in the back of the room, but there was nothing from the people up front, who were so glued to the TV screen (another parallel between children and old people) that they probably thought my playing was part of the soundtrack.

Wanda had been wheeled close to me by a nurse, and now she ordered in my ear, "Play somethin' they know."

So I did something bold—I got to my feet, crossed to the television set, and turned the volume all the way down. A few people stared at me in wounded confusion, as if they'd just been slapped. I walked purposefully back to the piano, sat down again, and with as much feeling as I could began playing a song from 1942 called "Moonlight Becomes You." It's from *Road to Morocco*, one of my favorite Bing Crosby and Bob Hope films, something I thought an audience born in the teens of the last century would recognize.

No "shut ups" now. People stirred and gazed toward the music. From the corner of my eye, I saw one man wheel his chair a little closer. Wanda was tapping her leg and swaying back and forth with her eyes closed, moving to the rhythm of this bluesy song that was a hit when she was young. When I reached the end, I started the song again so that the moment could continue for them.

Nurses had paused in their work and come to the dining room door to listen. As I finished, one of them whispered, "Play another one!" I felt many expectant eyes on me as I racked my brain for more music from bygone eras. *Don't draw a blank now, Lucy, not now! Come on, this is your chance to save everyone! For a moment, at least.*

"Moonlight Serenade," made famous by Glenn Miller and His Orchestra in 1944, came to the rescue. It was beautiful to see those faces responding to music they knew and, I hoped, being transported back to happy moments lying dormant inside them. When I finished playing, I went back to the television set and turned the volume up again, too loudly thanking everyone for allowing me to play. Except for the nurses warmly thanking me, nobody said a word. I could sense the people drifting back down, disappearing into the shadows of their current reality again. As I wheeled a beaming Wanda out the doors and into the hall, they stared after us.

I helped Wanda to her bathroom so she could freshen up and *tinkle*, as she called peeing. She had tons of funny slang sayings. She always referred to having to urinate as "not bein' able to hold her puckerin' string." Today she insisted on going into the bathroom alone, embarrassed by her faulty puckerin' string. "It don't work no more," she told me.

I waited outside the bathroom door in case she needed help. Then I got her situated in her spot for filming and asked if she needed anything before we continued.

"More lipstick," she said, and although she didn't have much lip, really, she reapplied her red pout. I turned on the camera, and off we went.

Lucy: How far did you get in school?

Wanda: Sophomore in high school.

Lucy: And then what happened?

Wanda: I went an' got married the first time. I was right around in that region, an' in that age group, an' that's what I did. In those days, why, they didn't pay attention to your age, your kids, nothin' else. I just went along an' got married not even outta high school an' thought at the time, "Well, I'm just the smartest gal that ever thought or been." That wasn't true, but, well, I'm sharper than most people, at least. I'll give the good Lord thanks for what he's helped me with to think right up here, right up here [pointing to her head].

Because most of these people here at the nursin' home don't know nothin', an' they did go to school. That one talks to herself, an' talks to herself, an' talks to herself, an' there's many others that's just as mad as she is. An' you just get so used to it, you just think, "At least the education I got has helped me more in old age than them, because they're talkin' about their high school days an' their graduation, an' look how they ended up." The good Lord left me with my sensibility. I can think faster than any of 'em women down here. They just let it slide by, let their minds slip away. I don't do that.

I try to help the people here, I go to the bathrooms an' pick up all of the rubble, I clean the toilet stool, I do a lot of things. I come to my room an' do the same thing, because I was brought up that way, the good Lord knows I was. So I try not to offend the Lord, an' he tries not to offend me. But it's impossible to not feel offended, with so many wheelchairs, wheelchairs, wheelchairs...an' so many people in 'em that don't give a pip about their mind anymore, they don't give a pip. They came here for one good reason, an' that's to be waited on hand an' foot until they die. I don't believe that way.

I believe you've got to help yourself until the end in whatever you partake in, you've got to do that. If you don't, you might just as well throw in the towel, because people watchin' think that much less of you in the long run. An' you don't want 'em to think you're less, because some of 'em get real nasty mean, just downright mean when they think you're helpless.

See, I worked at the Champaign County Nursin' Home for three years every weekend in the dinin' room, so I know how to deal with people. I've always known that. An' I worked at the junior high in Urbana as a supervisor for eight years [which was embarrassing for my mom while she was a student there]. I worked at the sports stadium in the kitchen for eight years. I worked at the assembly hall….

I knew Wanda had worked as a cook in a nursing home, running the dining room, and the irony of it caught me in the throat. I thought of Shakespeare's words in *As You Like It*: "All the world's a stage, and all the men and women merely players. They have their exits and their entrances; and one man in his time plays many parts…." In life's awesome cyclical nature, we step into the shoes of those who preceded us. Wanda had once cared for the very old, and now she was very old and needing care herself.

Wanda: I worked everywhere there was people. An' I loved it, I loved it, an' I love people. I love to mingle with 'em, an' joke, an' talk to 'em. That's what people need, to talk. People really need help, every way, shape, an' form, so I try to fill in. But I see that most people don't think that way, they don't think that way at all.

Lucy: Most people in the world don't think that way.

Wanda: They just think of their own aches an' pains, that's what they think of. That's not fair to the other guy next to you. That's not fair to me, that's not fair to you, if you was in the same boat—see, it's not fair to nobody. But see, it runs that way because there's not two minds that work the same, there's not two minds alike. I love most people, most of 'em I can get along with.

Take, for instance, today at that dinin' room lunch table, those three people that I introduced you to, Millie an' George an' Bill…they've come in here an' they don't turn their hands to nothin'. They expect it done for 'em. I come to my table, an' every day the staff has got my stuff throwed down, throwed down. I place everythin' just the way I want—I get my salt, pepper, sugar, what have you…put it in nice clean order. The others set right there an' stare at me all the time I'm doin' things for myself. They don't do nothin' for theirselves. George is the only one that really helps me. Millie don't help me, an' Bill don't help me. So I help myself an' us all, because I was brought up that way an' that's the way I'm goin' to live until I'm six foot under, I'm goin' to live that way.

An' them wheelchairs—the biggest nuisance that ever thought of bein', an' here I am in one. I give room for other people's chairs…I make room for 'em, but they just sit an' let somebody else push 'em here/there, here/there, here/there. An' most of 'em talk to theirself all the time…what's that gon' do for me?? Nothin', nothin'. I've got to do for myself an' for the people I can help, that's what I'm gon' do. I know what the score is.

An' when some of them nurses' aides get smarty, I get smart right back, because there's no point to it. Two of 'em come in this morning, just slammin' stuff…slam your shoes down, slam your clothes down. I wouldn't even have them two characters as a gift if they was given to me. I don't live that way, an' I don't like it.

There are good ones, too, though. My head nurse is the sweetest thing. She tells me to think happy things at bedtime an' she brings me a little candy drop to put in my mouth to try an' sleep. She's real good at lovin'

me an' I love her dearly. I love Julie, Angie, Lisa, Lisa…
there's two Lisas I love…an' they love me, they say.
Every day they come to me an' say, "How you doin',
Wanda, we think about you constantly." A nurse name
Tiny is the one who does all the what-fors an' the why-
fors for all of us livin' here, an' she brings me sweet
treats, too. Tiny kisses me every time she comes, she's
got personality streamin' out her whole body.

I focus on the good ones, see, 'cause if I'm goin' to
be confined here 'til my dyin' day, I want to be at least
a little bit loose an' a little bit good for people. I don't
want to be a horse's neck. I don't want to be that.

Lucy: That's so inspiring, as a young person, to hear
you say these things.

Wanda: Oh, sure, it helps anybody, hon, it helps
anyone.

And then, pulled by unseen forces, Wanda jumped
to a completely unrelated topic before taking another
breath….

CHAPTER SEVEN

Wanda: An' now Kathy lives at a house for special people. She's got 'em over there like I've got 'em right here. She calls me every day, every day, every day. She's a good little girl. She's never dated a man, an' I hope she never does, because some men is unforgivable an' worthless, but that's not her fault. She's a good little girl, an' there she is in Champaign at a home, an' here I am at a home. Because, well....

Kathy and men. Warm-up to a tough topic. Did I have the courage to finally ask?

Lucy: Do you like the home she's in?
Wanda: I've only been there a few times.
Lucy: Does she seem happy?
Wanda: She seems to be, she seems to be. She goes on trips with the gang, there's about six or seven of 'em go at a time, which seems to help her. But the city is notorious right now, some guys had broken in...one woman was takin' a shower, an' they just busted right in on her, I heard it this mornin' on TV...an' things like that happen, an' I think about Kathy constantly... just think what could happen, hon, think what could happen if one of them men...an' there's men right there at the house where she lives, an' I worry about that constantly.

With this second comment about Kathy and men,

I realized we had arrived—it was time to ask about the one thing. I'd carried harsh judgment against my grandparents about this one thing for years now. Even though I was chomping at the bit to hear what I assumed would be Wanda's heartfelt admission, I spoke evenly, careful not to put any weight on my words.

Lucy: Didn't Kathy have a bad sexual experience with a man, in high school?

Wanda: Well, she don't think too much about it anymore. I always say, "Kathy, be mighty careful, it pays to be careful." The little soul needs so much. She loves me, an' I love her dearly.

Whoa. She had dodged the question and was gazing at me in silence. My shock had me at a loss for the first time during our interview. Unknown to Wanda, I already knew the details of what she was attempting to breeze past. It was a big fat protected confidence in my family that my Aunt Kathy had had only one sexual experience in her life, and it was when she was raped in the empty high school auditorium in her senior year. The boy was in special ed with Kathy, as were the several other kids who looked on from nearby. A member of the school staff stumbled upon this happening, and the school called my grandparents immediately.

The first thing the adults did after they got Kathy home was attempt to determine if the deed had been consensual or if the boy had in fact raped her. Wanda and Dale were too uncomfortable to confront her them-selves, so they made Jody do it. My sixteen-year-old mom sat seventeen-year-old Kathy on her bed and asked her the very personal and necessary questions.

Kathy always had a hard time conversing; she was vague and unfocused. So my mom had to be direct and graphic with her questions, to which Kathy was not vague at all in her insistence that the act had not been consensual. My mom reported this to the adults, but Kathy was never taken to the hospital for any medical examination or treatment. Cue the beginnings of my judgment, which would only escalate from there.

Kathy was immediately pulled from school, and the waiting game began...Was she pregnant? My grandfather barely slept for days, my mom remembers, sitting up nights in his armchair. Finally, Kathy got her period. And still, Dale and Wanda did not go to the authorities; they did not press charges. The rape remained a secret, more or less.

It had happened just a few months shy of graduation, and while Kathy was able to graduate, she did not have to attend the ceremony. Or more truthfully put, her graduation experience was taken from her, along with all the other things that rape steals. My mom, on the other hand, had to see the accused boy in the halls every day and pretend like everything was fine. Life seemingly moved on.

Now. I have never been a victim of rape, thank God, nor had a child who was. Let me tell you, the searing heat of my adolescent judgment toward my grandparents was in how the *entire thing* went down. First, my teenage mom having to ask the questions—just no, that's not appropriate for a minor to try to handle. Second, Kathy not receiving proper medical attention.

Third, the boy not being punished by law (if at all). And don't even get me started on the bystander apathy of those teenage onlookers. Fourth, Kathy having to miss out on her graduation, after she had worked so hard to do well in school.

Yes, the last could have been viewed as what was best for her, and she might have even been relieved, but the fact is, she was demoted to the shadows while the boy stayed in school and attended graduation ceremonies in the light. I suppose he may not have been punishable because of his disabilities; but still. And I have to assume that Wanda and Dale, perhaps like most parents then, truly did not know what to do or what was available to them, and felt that keeping it quiet and hoping for the best seemed like their only option.

But there was also the underlying embarrassment: In their small community, seeking justice for their daughter on a public scale would've rocked Dale and Wanda's world even further. It takes immense courage to come forward, for both a victim and their loved ones, and sometimes we choose not to because we don't see how it will do any good after the fact. It's too painful, and the human reaction to pain is to reject it and forget as quickly as possible.

Unfortunately, in brushing the rape under the rug, they may have inadvertently added to the trauma that had already rocked Kathy's life, with or without justice. If they lacked the capacity to handle asking her the sensitive questions at the time, how on earth could they have helped her talk about how she felt in the weeks, months, and years afterward? Setting an example of

REMEMBER ME AS HUMAN

silence causes victims, particularly minors, to follow suit, when in fact what they might need most is the creation of a safe way in which to communicate their feelings about what happened. Kathy went along with the incident being shut down and never spoke about it again. Rape is a shameful and confusing wound to carry, whether in public or in secret, and she carried it for the rest of her life.

As I sat there, not quite sure what to say next, Wanda casually continued to veer away from the subject of Kathy's rape.

Wanda: I wonder about her food, an' what she eats, an' how she gets by. I wonder 'bout a whole bunch of things, Lucy, I wonder. She'll soon be sixty next month. I still save all my Bingo goodies an' prizes for when she comes down here to visit me…candy bars, potato chips, cookies, all that stuff. She always wants to know what I saved for her, an' I tell her, "Honey, you don't need to worry, I've saved plenty for you." An' she says, "I love you, Mom, I love you." An' I say, "I love you, too." That's what we've got goin'.

In that moment, I realized that this was not about bringing my grandmother an awakening. The awakening was for me. I saw how people defend their choices at all cost, how we shield ourselves from our past mistakes. Wanda was unwilling to confront her daughter's rape, even now. At this ripe old age, she had no intention of venturing out of the shallows into the depths of uncomfortable memories. She was no different from the rest of us, I suppose, who bend the past so we can live with ourselves. I guess that's just being human.

Kathy lived with her mother right up until Wanda went into the nursing home. When that happened, Kathy was moved into a group home, with other people who had special needs. There, through a work program, she had her first steady jobs. When she talked about working and being paid, she would beam with pride. Having a purpose expanded her life exponentially, and she thrived.

For a time, Kathy had a pet dog, after one of the staff members took her to purchase it without asking her family first. Oh, lord. She had always been crazy in love with animals, but she was not able to care for one of her own, and so the dog was ultimately taken away. I know this was devastating for her, and just as devastating for my mom and my cousin, who were forced to be the bad guys in the situation. Kathy lived in the group home for six years after Wanda's death, until she died from sepsis on October 29, 2017, at the age of sixty-seven.

The bottom line is, I will never know exactly what my grandparents thought and felt about the choices they made after Kathy's rape, and I've decided it's none of my business. I don't need to have an opinion either way. Only compassion remains, for all of them. I know Wanda and Dale struggled with what they thought was right and did the best they could. If we live into our nineties, we too may be unwilling to peer into a few old closets.

By this point, I had lost my train of thought, but I

steadied my voice and kept the interview moving... moving back in time.

Lucy: What was the best date Grandpa Dale ever took you on?

Wanda: Dale an' I both worked at a place called The Inn in Urbana. He worked the fillin' station out in front, an' I waited tables inside. He worked durin' the daytime, an' me at night...so he would go to bed an' sleep, an' then get up an' pick me up after I got off work. We'd get in his little ol' Ford car, which gassed you almost to death inside, an' we'd head for the neighborin' towns of Danville an' Westville. We'd go see floor shows there an' what have you, just enjoy ourselves. People there were known to have all-night activity, that's what it was made for.

Lucy: What's a floor show?

Wanda: Oh, live entertainment of all sorts...singers, dancers, comedians, in a nightclub-type place. We just loved that stuff.

Lucy: How did Dale catch your eye?

Wanda: Oh, I never even thought too much about him at all, because I was busy waitin' those tables an' we had quite a clientele to keep up with. So I never thought too much about him, until he started askin' me to date him when I got off work.

Lucy: Did you think he was sexy?

Wanda: I thought he was a nice-lookin' fella, which he always was. Both my husbands was very handsome, very handsome. The first one had the curliest hair, just laid in massive waves. An' he was good-lookin'. An' then Dale come along, an' his had just one big wave across the front, enough to make him look real handsome, which he was. An' Dale had different features than the first one, completely. His nose was bigger an', uh, all different things stood out in him that I didn't care for in my first husband. An' besides, Dale made no casting remarks about other women like Henry did. Henry just always was tryin' to rile my jealousy up. Well, I had jealousy in me, because my father was always very jealous of my mother, very much so.

Lucy: Did your dad have a reason to be jealous of your mom?

Wanda: Well, no, except for her outgoin' personality. He didn't care for that. He was very different, bein' from England, an' he just thought, "She can refrain from all that, the way she is with her own relations." But she had it in her veins to be that way, she could not help herself. She just stated however she felt an' whenever, an' he was jealous of her, very, very touchy. He'd come right out…maaaaannnnn, it wouldn't make any difference where they were at, an' ball her out, ball her out. Say, "You didn't have to do that, that was a no-no." But Mom would say, "Frank, I'm made that way an' I'm gonna stay that way." So that's what she did, that's what she did.

Lucy: Was Dale romantic?

Wanda: Oh, yeah, oh, yeah, full-tilt. We always had our romancin', full-tilt. We went with each other a year an' then we got married. He was very good to me, he meant well. But now, the romance is gone. I barely even have visitors. Heavens, those people that I introduced you to in the dinin' room? They have half their family at every meal. I lay right there in that bed an' cry myself to sleep every night, every night. It really burns my fanny.

Lucy: Why didn't you move to California with us?

Wanda: I don't want to disrupt your homes, didn't wanna do that. I don't care for livin' in California anyway, I wouldn't want to. It's "life in the fast lane" out there, an' I, uh, I never got that point, never did, never did. I just took it a day at a time or a night at a time here in Illinois, because that's the way I had to do. Since Dale went an' got that horrible disease, an' now he's gone…I have to stay close to where he is now, an' that's here.

Lucy: If you had a choice, what would you do?

Wanda: I certainly wouldn't be right here, I'd be outta this pea patch.

Lucy: Where do you want to be?

Wanda: In a regular assisted-livin' home, that's what I'd like. It didn't turn out that way an' here I am down here.

Lucy: I think if you're angry, you should talk about moving somewhere else.

Wanda: Don't do a bit of good. I've been able to get through it so far where I'm at, but it's a shame it turned out this way.

This was so tough to hear. I knew that Wanda had already chosen to be here when she called my mom to make the move, and that it was the best of the homes available—smaller, with more attention given. I knew my cousin Talor, with her own family and career, visited as often as she could, but she was pretty much Wanda's only nearby support. Every comforting thing I thought to say immediately seemed stupid and naive. I suddenly felt totally unequipped in the face of such loneliness.

There was a real reason my grandparents' money had dried up to the point where Wanda was living here instead of in assisted living, and it involved one of our family members close to her. The situation was confusing and complex when it happened, shrouded in a mess of lies. All I will say on this public scale is that old people are extremely vulnerable to vultures and thieves, especially when they're in the family. Sitting with Wanda that day, I felt too young, too uninformed, and too timid to get involved, though keeping my mouth shut was painful. If it were now, I would feel insanely confident in taking a full-force stand for her, not only fighting to put her money back where it belonged but getting her living where she preferred to be, as I would go on to do for my paternal grandfather years later. I so wish I had been able to. *I'm sorry, Grandma.*

As she steered so many of the questions I asked her right back to her living situation, I felt foolish for waltzing in with my carefree youth, and debased by the harsh reality of having to end your time on earth in a home that's not yours. My respect for Wanda and *all elders* having to endure their final years like this was overwhelming.

Wanda was becoming visibly distressed, so I cut the camera. I couldn't bear to upset her any further, and as

I got her a drink of water, I offered to end the interview for today.

"No, no," she said, "I'd like to keep goin' a little more."

Little did I know that the path we ventured down next would prove even more difficult to handle.

Lucy: Tell me about Dale's parents.

Wanda: Dale's mom Marie broke her hip an' she died from it. She was a good woman, Dale's mother, my mother-in-law. An' Dale's dad...he was an old frisky man. Couldn't keep his hands off of a woman, couldn't keep 'em off.

Remember I mentioned a darker side to Clinton?

Lucy: Was he ever inappropriate with you?

Wanda: Oh, certainly, he tried to rape me right in his office downtown. Old Man Boyer tried to rape me while Dale was overseas in the service durin' World War Two. I was very vulnerable, left alone with two small kids when Dale was drafted.

Lucy: How did you get away?

Wanda: I called him a little bit of everythin' nasty an' said, "You lay a hand on me again an' you have had it."

She was leaning all the way forward in her wheelchair, almost teetering on the edge of it, engrossed in recounting the story with high drama in her eyes. I stared at her in disbelief as she continued.

Wanda: He came at me real strong, tryin' to get on top of me on the desk, an' then backin' me into a corner, but I ran clear to the door of his office an' maaaaaaan,

I laid him out cold with my words. I said, "You...you got the wrong person." I said, "What would you think if I wrote my husband a nice long letter tellin' him that you tried to rape me right up in your office here at the grain elevator?" That's what I told him. An' then he—"

"Need some ice?"

We both jumped a mile as an abrupt male voice interrupted from the doorway. A very large attendant had popped his head in and broken the spell of Wanda's nail-biting story. I couldn't help glaring at him. *Dammit, man, shit timing.* I was hangry. Aside from pushing lunch around in its compartmentalized tray, I hadn't eaten since the night before, and I was feeling that aggressive animalistic edge. Spewing silent poison at him with my eyes, I forced pleasantry from my lips.

"I don't know, do you need ice, Grandma?"

Wanda was gazing at him strangely. "Yeah, please," she mouthed.

"Where's the ice bucket?" came the abrupt guy again.

Where's the ice bucket? Look around this tiny room and find it, for the love of God, that's your job.

"Here you are, sir," I said cheerfully as I rose from the bed and grabbed the beige plastic thing from the bedside table, where it was easily visible. All the while I kept my eyes on Wanda and kept speaking to her. "That's really intense what you're telling me, Grandma."

I was trying to keep her in the zone, but she was not focused on recounting her narrow escape from her father-in-law. She was suspiciously eyeing the ice-bucket guy as he noisily refilled her bucket a few feet away.

"I don't like him, I don't like him at all," she whisper-yelled.

He clearly heard her, and I had to cover my laughter with a theatrical cough. "Thank you, thank you," I rushed him, offering a smile of apology for her rude words.

"Yup," he muttered as he lumbered out of the room, shaking his head.

Hell, I thought, she was saying no worse than what had gone through my head, only I kept my thoughts silent and she blurted hers out. It must come with age, the disregard for social graces that were considered so necessary in youth.

With the two of us on our own again, I pulled Wanda's focus back to the experience she'd been in the middle of recounting. I had to hear what happened next with my Great-Grandfather Clinton.

Lucy: So, Grandma, you were telling me about Dale's dad trying to rape you in his office.

Wanda: Yes. An' for a long time after Dale Boyer come home from the service, I never told him a single thing about his father. I never told him a single thing until he got me real ticked off, an' then I said, "Listen, you go to your father"...I said, "You go to your father, an' you ask him what took place in his office. An' he better tell you the truth, or I will."

Lucy: So when Dale asked his dad about the attempted rape, did Old Man Boyer admit it?

Wanda: Well, we had to take Dad Boyer up to the hospital for his bladder, after Dale got home from the war. An' when we went to bring him home, Mom Boyer an' I were waitin' alone in the car, an' she said to me, "I cannot take care of Pop by myself." I said, "I'll stay a few days an' help you." Of course, he had already tried all his sexual maneuvers on me, an' I thought, "You just try it again, baby, an' I'll sock you right square in that big fat Boyer nose."

Then when Dale an' I dropped his parents back at their farm, I said, "I'm gonna stay for a while, Dale, an' help your mother with your dad." An' he got very mad, because I had told him about his father's tryin' junk on me. An' he said, "I don't think you need to do that." I said, "I'm doin' it for your mother's sake, not for your poppa, you keep that in mind." Old Man Boyer was a son of a gun, absolutely a son of a gun. Dale's brothers an' sisters shoulda known the half of it about their pop, about all his maneuvers...but they didn't, they didn't.

Or did they? While I have heard from some of those now-grown relatives that they really loved the poetry-and-tea lap time with the family patriarch, I've also heard from others less enthusiastic. Being pulled onto Clinton's lap was not an enjoyable experience for everyone. My mom confided that as a young girl, she learned to steer clear of her Grandfather Clinton and his lap. He would try to take her hand and guide her, and she would yank free and run. Even at a young age, she says, she felt he "wasn't right in that way."

What my mom has alluded to for a long time is that Clinton molested several children in the family. It is a fact that has been confirmed by the survivors, whose privacy I respect. I know this is painful and confusing for both sides, those loyal to Clinton and those harmed by him. While it's all ancient history, one thing is clear: The lovely little slice of generational drama has never been openly discussed.

As playwright John Patrick Shanley once said to me, "Everybody doesn't talk about something, right?" I don't know about everybody, but in past generations of my family, difficult things like molestation, along with alcoholism, suicide, and mental illness, of which we have all of the above, have not been willingly acknowledged. As with most (all?) families on the planet, we have had an unspoken agreement not to get too close to certain issues. Painful happenings are tucked deep down in the dark places and kept there, young and old alike. If my Great-Grandma Marie was aware of her husband's misdeeds, she stayed by his side all his days regardless.

As Wanda recalled her traumatizing past with her father-in-law, she was starting to take longer and longer pauses, and I could feel her concentration straining.

Lucy: All right, Grandma, we're going to end our talk there for today....

As she stared into space, "Grandma, I'm going to end the interview for today," I repeated more loudly and stood up. She looked up at me in a fog and seemed to struggle with where she was. I knelt down at her wheelchair and gently told her, "You did a great job today, you can rest now."

I knew the interview had stirred up a lot, and now

it was swirling inside her with nowhere to go. I felt a bit guilty in hoping she would save it for the next day, right there below the surface.

I was exhausted, too, but my day's work was far from over. I needed to go photograph the place where so many of these stories began: the Roughton family farm. Before I kissed her goodbye, I asked her how to get to the spot where her old house had been, and though her directions were mostly landmarks, trees, and fences, I did my best to interpret them into my notebook. Since Wanda hadn't grown up with addresses and now had none to give me, I was going to have to find the spot the old-fashioned way.

CHAPTER EIGHT

LIVING IN LOS ANGELES, I was used to directions given in terms of minutes, moving either toward or away from the beach, as opposed to here in the endless flatlands, where they were given in miles and by the compass. Wanda's sense of direction was impeccable, from having lived down unmarked roads and following the path of the sun all her life. All humans possess this innate sense of direction, but those of us who spend our lives in cement jungles, who've become numbed and dumbed by technology, have lost and forgotten it. I even find myself automatically following the map home when I already know the way, so addicted to having an ETA. Our brains have become stupid and lazy, one app at a time. People Wanda's age were creatures from a different era—before the insanity of being glued to a phone, when human connection was felt in a deeper way; when moments moved at a pace that was slow enough to feel, and basic survival skills like a sense of direction were unimpaired.

I set out from the nursing home about three, racing the sun before it fell on these short winter days. Amazingly, Wanda's abstract directions made perfect sense, every fork in the road, every boulder where she said it would be…the woman knew this countryside by heart. After about thirty-five minutes following landmarks (there I go again with the minutes), I came up alongside the three hundred and fifty acres of farmland (according to her) that Wanda's father had owned and farmed from the turn of the last century to 1940, when he died.

I sped up with anticipation as I saw the farm come into view, and then I was upon it, a white two-story house and half a dozen outbuildings. I knew these were not the original buildings; the house and barns had been torn down in the late seventies.

Before I neared the front of the property, I veered onto the gravel shoulder with enough distance so as not to alarm the current tenants. People in these isolated communities noticed everyone who came and went, and a stranger stopping would put them on high alert. I assumed there were at this very moment unseen eyes checking me out from behind drawn curtains.

With my camera around my neck, I got out and walked a ways into the empty field across the road from the house. From that distance, I got a panoramic view of the property, fields stretching to dense trees. Whoever lived here now had a quirky sense of humor: They had their yard decorated with glass bottles, funny bird feeders, and life-size jungle animals, all painted bright colors. I sat down on the cold dirt, unsure of what to do next. *Take photographs*, I reminded myself, and shot a few. As I sat in silence, sensations of the earth rose to meet me: birds gossiping in the trees, the lazy wind carrying voices of memories over the plain, the mild warmth of the fading sun, the smell of manure.

I gazed out across the dim expanse, amazed that so much of my ancestors' lives had taken place here. The vibrant experiences Wanda conveyed of her early life on this very spot danced through my imagination. When the original house was torn down, its entire skeleton had been buried in a huge shallow grave dug in the side yard. Even from across the road, I could see the pockmarks in the ground where it lay. How wild that new families walked over it, unaware of the past and what it had meant to those who came before.

Life on earth has always been unfolding and imploding back on itself, entire civilizations come and go, yet we live in our little reality aware only of what exists before our eyes. We can't see all that stood before, but we certainly can feel it. Sensitive beings, we are pushed and pulled as we intermingle with layers of the past. How many buried houses, villages, kingdoms have we walked over? Ever get a specific feeling when you come into a space, positive or negative? Sometimes a place makes me so dizzy, I have to sit down. Wherever you are right now, take a moment to think about what could've happened on that very spot.

Sitting across from the Roughton farmland, I began to sink into the weight of my family's invisible past. Love, hate, grief, joy, pleasure, pain, laughter, tears, fear, courage…the Roughtons' life here had brought years of turbulent ups and downs; and now all the cards had been dealt, the hands had been played, the deck forgotten.

I spoke absentmindedly into the whipping wind. "Ashes to ashes, dust to dust"—the phrase suddenly made sense to me, in a way it had not in all the years of Sundays I'd heard it said in Catholic mass. Now, sitting in the middle of nowhere, it finally became personal. Nothing matters at all, and yet, everything matters completely; life is a total and utter contradiction. What had happened here had meant the world to those it happened to, and now not a single soul who remembered it was alive except for Grandma. When she died, all memory of this place as it was would be lost forever.

Sure, I could learn it as best I could and preserve it by writing it down, but the actual living memories would be gone. Our pathetic recordings of history are but shadow puppets against the light of experience. And time, that relentless force, flows on, carrying away with it the stories of countless lives. I guess that's the fear I've been running from, with all the documenting, the asking…the fear of being swept away by time.

Such jumbled emotions I felt all at once: relief that I had made it to Wanda in time, panic that I would never be able to preserve all she remembered. My long-standing personal grudge against Alzheimer's still raged inside me. I had a strong urge to drive straight back to Grandma and continue talking about her life all night long. But I came to terms with something really important in that moment: Even if we talked for the rest of the year, there would always be stories I'd never know.

"Can you live with that?" the wind asked. "Enough," I answered. *Enough. Tomorrow.*

As I walked back to the road, I photographed the farm from various closer angles. The sun had settled behind the distant horizon, blanketing the land in icy blue twilight. I took one last picture of the scarred grass under which the house Wanda grew up in was entombed, waved at whoever might be studying me from the windows, and ran to the warmth of the car.

————————

FOR THE NEXT TWO nights, I'd be staying with my cousin Talor, her husband, Tim, and their teenage son, Mason. Talor and I share our birthday and our grandparents. Talor and Tim began dating in high school, and they have gone on to have a beautiful lifelong marriage. They are fourteen years older than me, and I proudly admit that Tim was my first love.

I remember Talor and Tim going to the prom when I was five years old. At that age, I had a habit of running full speed at people to hug them. This was an awkward situation for men, as I was oblivious to the fact that my face was hitting them directly in the crotch. I was crazy about Tim, and wanted to hug-rush him constantly. Years later we all laughed around the dinner table about how uneasy he'd felt when I'd face-plant him in his privates.

Talor and Tim married when I was seven, and I was the flower girl in their wedding. I was so overjoyed to be standing close to Tim up there at the altar. Annoyingly, I was under strict instruction not to hug-rush him under any circumstance.

Talor had asked my mom to sing "Loving You" during the ceremony, but my mom was too nervous to sing it live. Instead, she recorded the song a few weeks earlier, and it was played over the speakers as Talor walked down the aisle. Jody herself will tell you that it is absolutely typical of her to not want to sing in public. Her best friend, Gladys, asked her to sing at her wedding, and again, my mom declined. If there were two people in this life my mom would do anything for, it's Talor and Gladys—that's how much she hates being front-and-center.

Funny, Jody did not move to Los Angeles at twenty-one to be a singer, but when fate has a plan, who are we to question it? She performed in several benefit concerts for the Santa Barbara Bowl and recorded vocals on two hit songs: Joe Walsh's "Life's Been Good," 1978 (if you know her way of speaking, you can hear her signature s's on the "He's cool" line), and Dan Fogelberg's "There's a Place in the World for a Gambler," 1974, which was featured in the Olympics that year.

She also did not move to L.A. intending to meet my dad, but fate had that in store as well. Back in Urbana, my mom was friends with two guys who would go on to rule the music business: Bob Nutt and Irving Azoff. They had been running a booking agency for bands out of Bob's house, and when they expanded to L.A. to start an artist-management company, they told my mom if she ever wanted to join them, she'd have a job as their secretary.

She kept it in the back of her mind while she worked and went to junior college, majoring in English, until her boyfriend, a musician, pitched the idea of taking Bob and Irving up on their offer. Boyfriend's plan was that she would move to L.A. and pave the way with connections for him for when he joined her within a few months. A gorgeous country ingénue ready to experience the world's delights, Jody asked her mom to cash out her insurance policy and used the eighty-five dollars to buy a one-way ticket to her future.

It was Mama's first time on an airplane, and when she saw those L.A. palm trees from the window, she says, she knew she'd never go back. She took the job in the music business and she made connections, all right, they just weren't going to benefit Boyfriend.

Enter my dad, Joe Walsh. With his first bands, Barnstorm and James Gang, he was one of Irving and Bob's early clients, and the story is that when my mom was part of a group picking him and his band up at the airport on one of her first assignments, he fell hard. She tried to cling to her loyalty for Boyfriend, but she was smitten, too, and a few weeks later, when Joe walked up to her in a crowded greenroom and presented her with roses, word quickly got back to Boyfriend that the only way that would be paved for him was to heartbreak. Although my dad was involved in a relationship, too, they eventually cleared the way for one another and stayed together for eleven years, married for the last five.

It was a very painful loss for both of them when they fell apart, and although I was too young to remember the divorce, my mom says I definitely showed signs of distress. Just old enough to stand, I would take all my clothes out of my drawers and put them in a pile on my bedroom floor. I have to think it was because I saw my dad packing and I copied his behavior, wanting to go, too. To this day, a feeling of homesickness washes over me whenever I'm packing or folding laundry.

As my mom dreamed of someone more interested in raising a family than my dad had been, her friends

Kenny and Eva Loggins introduced her to a man named Jim Recor. Jim was also in the music business. He was Kenny's tour manager and longtime friend; he also co-wrote several Fleetwood Mac songs and worked with them on the business side. Jim had a daughter a year older than me, Alison, and he and Jody not only hit it off but bonded over their desire to create a family for their young daughters. They tied the knot when I was three; their wedding is one of my earliest memories. Grace arrived when I was four, Spencer when I was six, and together we have been the most loving and devoted family I ever could have wished for. My absolute heart, my everything.

BEING IN THE CHURCH dressing room with Talor as she prepared for the ceremony, with women bustling all around getting her ready, was thrilling. They all clucked like chickens and snapped at one another, each vying to be most important to the bride.

Even I got primped by my mom for my appearance down the church aisle. My fancy dress was white with black polka dots and a black-velvet sash; I had a white flower wreath on my head. My fourteenth-century pageboy haircut and pantyhose that drooped in the crotch to my knees didn't dampen my confidence in the slightest. Sitting up high in a makeup chair at a brightly lit vanity, I felt like a Star.

As my mom blushed my cheeks and told me for the hundredth time to pull my tights up, I rehearsed how my walk would go in my head. Unfortunately, I would be pulling my uncooperative little sister, an identically dressed flower girl, by the hand. She definitely didn't share my passion for making this performance go right, simply glared at everyone with her finger in her mouth and a corner of her red handkerchief stuffed up her nose. (This was an obsessive habit until she broke her arm and the cast kept her from reaching her nose.) Grace resisted practicing our walk, but I was not going to let her interfere with our mission, so I pulled her back and forth until it was time for the show to start.

Cousin Talor looked like a queen as she glided down the long aisle in her elaborate lace wedding dress. It had huge puffed sleeves, the Victorian kind that had a comeback in the eighties and were gone again by the nineties. Her hair was crinkled and teased within an inch of its life into a classic up-do, and she was beaming with excitement and love. During the wedding procession, (perfectly) led by *moi* and cranky Grace, my mom blushed in the pews as her beautiful voice hit those high notes from the safety of the recording: "Loving you has made my life so beautiful, do do do do do, ahhhhhhhhh."

I guess I knew I wasn't the main event, but I took my part very seriously. As they say in acting, "There are no small roles." After all, it was I who would set the stage for the whole shebang, and if I messed up, it would ruin the entire wedding. It was life or death in my mind. The intoxicating excitement I'd felt in the dressing room is how I still feel when I'm backstage about to perform. Since that day, I've been addicted to the whole experience of preparing and performing, making everything go right for the audience and my fellow cast members. Or in a wedding, same thing. And I've never forgotten that there are no small roles.

I WAS NEARING TALOR and Tim's house, passing through a handful of small towns, just filling stations and cemeteries, really. I never could pass a moody cemetery without stopping, and even though the sky was now midnight blue with just a thin line of fiery orange at the horizon, I stopped the car at a little white church surrounded by headstones. Life and death seemed so much more intermingled here, so intriguing to a city girl. Back in Los Angeles, the land of eternal youth, we try to separate life and death completely. Our cemeteries, or "memorial parks," look like lush golf courses. Words like *graveyard, tombstone, funeral parlor* are considered macabre and off-topic. But in my grandparents' youth, people were born and died at home, caskets were open, the wake was in the living room, and the deceased was buried down the road in the family plot.

Visiting family in Illinois, a sheltered kid from the land of memorial parks, I'd have nightmares, psychologically overwhelmed by the prevalence of graveyards. Not wanting to offend the locals, who seemed totally unbothered by it all, I always made sure to keep my upset to myself, internalizing it in my dreams instead. I am still fascinated by graveyards, which I guess is why I now found myself alone in the dark in one. Striding between rows of two-hundred-year-old graves taking photographs, I suddenly felt like a crazy person. When I thought I saw a headstone move, I decided it was time to go. I walked calmly at first, but then lost my composure and sprinted back to the car.

When I arrived at Tim, Talor, and Mason's house, they were all waiting and welcomed me in with hugs and helping hands. "Sorry I'm late, I had to walk around in a graveyard in the dark like an absolute freak," I did *not* say out loud.

I had only my backpack to bring inside, but the men whisked it off to my room just the same. I'd be staying in their spare bedroom, in the black-iron bed that my grandparents slept in on their wedding night. It had been in the attic room of my grandfather's Boyer family farm.

I'd give anything for that bed, but of all the grandkids, that heirloom chose Talor. Talor's mom is my Aunt Susie, the first child Wanda and Dale had together, right before he left for the war. Susie is mentioned in every single one of her dad's letters home. Aunt Susie is still alive and well, living in Illinois, but I've never developed a relationship with her, aside from polite hugs at family get-togethers.

As Talor, Tim, Mason, and I ate dinner at the dining table, I was swept up in how much I adored these people. They're hilarious, kind, with a generosity to the skies, and beautifully nonjudgmental. Because of that open-mindedness, our conversations have the freedom to run deep, are thought-provoking, and always end positively, even though we come from different backgrounds and faiths.

After life updates and much laughter, it was kisses goodnight, and everyone went off to bed. The silence out here in the country was deafening. I felt lonely and a little lost, as the events of the day sank in. Reality had slipped slightly, and I was floating in between the lines, half here in the present, half spread out across the span of time back to Wanda's youth. There were voices, jumbled characters from the interview, stirring in my head. Because I didn't know most of the people Wanda had spoken of, not all of the voices had faces, but they were there, awakened from their long sleep and pulled to the surface. Now they wanted to be heard, their murmurs rising as I lay there.

It wasn't just voices from the stories but also from those silenced people in the nursing home. Now they clamored over one another, and because I had been careful not to look at them long, they were faceless, too. Did I really think I could handle this project, my own emotions, and the emotions of the people it involved?

Silence. Neglect. Last one living. Loneliness. Stop. Alcoholism. Abuse. Screaming. Can't sleep. Baby Donald couldn't swallow food. Grandpa couldn't remember. Buried houses. Molestation. Can't forget. Harold hit in the head with the swing. Graveyards. Can't sleep. Stop. Help me forget. Don't forget. Too loud. Don't leave us. Make it stop.

But I couldn't put back to sleep those I had awakened; it had gone too far, and I had to keep going. I had to make sense of it all for them, so their voices would be remembered. *Fuck you, Alzheimer's*. The bedside lamp cast a circle of soft light on the ceiling, and I lay on my back focusing my vision on it, hand over my heart. I do that when I'm anxious, feel for it beating. I figure as long as I can feel that life force, I'm okay, I must still be here for a reason. When the reason is gone, the heartbeat will cease.

Jesus, Lucy, not helpful right now. I sat up and took a sharp breath in. The voices would drive me crazy if I just lay there trying to ignore them. I buried myself in the task of transcribing a batch of Grandpa's letters into my laptop. The work drowned out the phantoms, and I spent the rest of the night with Dale in the year 1944. Yes, he was also a phantom, but at least he had a face.

My earliest Roughton ancestor, my Great-Great-Grandfather William, and his wife, Hannah. Originally from England, William carried this photo of Hannah while he fought in the Civil War.

Frank and Nellie Roughton,
Wanda's parents

Clinton and Marie Boyer,
Dale's parents

Wanda Roughton

Dale Boyer

Harold Roughton, 1922-1931

*One of the newspaper articles on
Harold's death, April 10, 1931*

*Harold's class photo. Harold is in the front row, far right.
The boy whose swing hit him in the head is in the back row, third
from right, with his face intentionally scratched out*

My Great-Grandfather Frank Roughton's suicide note, 1940

My grandparents at the Boyer farm on their wedding day in 1940

My husband, Will, and me on the same spot in 2022

Wanda and Dale on the day he left for the war, 1943

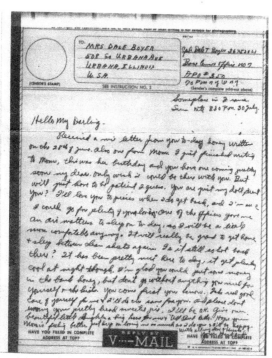

One of Dale's V-Mails, forwarded to his parents,
as Wanda was living with them for a time

No wonder Wanda talked about women going for the soldiers left and right. Dale sent this picture home in a letter, 1944

The war left Wanda at home with their two small children, Henry (from her first marriage) and Susie

Paris Area, France
Sat. Eve. 6:30 PM
3 Feb 1945

Hello My Darling -

I'm writing this from the office, I'm in charge of Quarters tonite, the fellow that had C.Q. wanted off so I told him I would take it. I'll get caught up on some of my letter writing maybe, getting my mail all at one time makes it a little hard to answer everybody right away + of course I'll write you if I don't anybody else. You come first always, you know that. Well I've been off to-day, but didn't do anything especially, tell Suzette I got her a nice bottle of perfume this afternoon + will send out another box in the near future, just as soon as I get

From the letter that Dale's spirit chose for me to read at his funeral

some more things gathered up, I know what I'll get for Susie & you but have to figure out something for Burk. But will have it on its way in a couple of days. I only hope you have received my Xmas box by now. It has been sent almost two months now, the way they handle boxes though it might have got all broken up, although I did have it packed & tied up good. I hope it has warmed up some back there honey the weather here has cleared up & warmed up till we hardly needed any fire to-day. But will probably break loose again before long. How is everybody at home sweetie? here I go again blowing off & never asked you how you were? I hope you are O.K. I'm just fine & was very happy to receive four nice letters from you, written on

Notice the bottom of page two/top of page three, where Dale mentions the date—the same as the day of his funeral

110

the 8th of Jan. I think you must have had
your dates mixed up a little, you were
writing on Sun. nite + Sun was the 7th, but
thats O.K. just so long as you write, another
on the 9th in fact two of the ninth, you are
just my doll for thinking about me + writing
so good + the last one on the 10th of Jan. The
one you wrote on Sun, you had been down
home all day, I'm sure glad you could
go down + I know the folks were plenty
glad to see you. Wish I could have been
there with you. The hunting sounds good,
but most of all I would want just you to
help with the hunting. Honey about the
pictures, I was going to have some taken
to-day, but the studio was closed, so will
have them taken the first of the week, it
takes about two weeks to get them back
here. But will send you one as soon as I
can. Am glad Macey got some from D.B.

Rebuilding after the war— Wanda at the drugstore where she worked

Dale at work for the Elks Club

Unexpected post-war blessings for Wanda and Dale: the births of my aunt Kathy (right), 1950, and my mom, Jody, 1952

Wanda and Dale settle into happy married life with their children;
from left: Jody, Susie, Kathy, Henry

My Aunt Kathy as a teenager, about the time
of the incident at her school

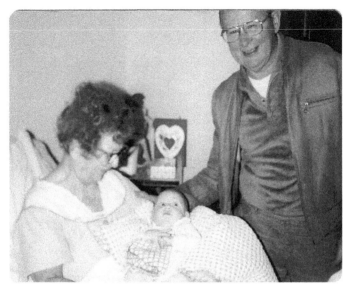

Enter ME: meeting my grandparents
Wanda and Dale for the first time, 1982

I love my grandpa's beaming face

With my Great-Grandma Marie Boyer, 1984

Me with Wanda and Dale, 1986

Grandma Wanda teaching me to play the piano

Me on the Boyer family farm, eight years old

*Cousin Talor's wedding to Tim and my role of a
lifetime as their flower girl*

From left: Aunt Kathy and me during our tattle-battle years, with Grandma Wanda, my sister Grace, Grandpa Dale, my mom Jody, my brother Spencer

Aunt Kathy

Wanda and Dale in Vermont
on my parents' farm, circa 1986

My Grandfather Dale and me at a family reunion, circa 1994

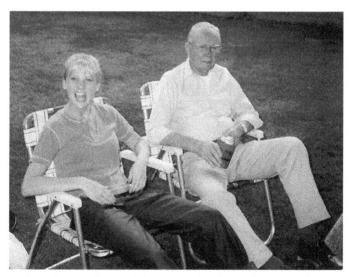

At gatherings, Dale could usually be found in a chair somewhere away from the commotion, and I usually sought him out

In 1990, my mom threw Wanda and Dale a huge
surprise party for their 50th wedding anniversary

Dale and Wanda about ten years later, when Dale was
almost completely taken by Alzheimer's

Wanda with another resident in the dining room of the nursing home, Valentine's Day, 2007

Wanda and Lucy at the nursing home, 2011

*Wanda at the keyboard during our interview
at the nursing home, 2011*

Finishing final rewrites on this book at Wanda and Dale's grave, 2023

CHAPTER NINE

I ARRIVED BACK AT the nursing home about nine a.m. Wanda was waiting to greet me in her favorite spot by the front doors, looking beautiful in her outfit of whites and pinks, her hair perfectly bubbled and sheened again, her makeup bright and bold. With rose-pink spectacles to match her get-up, the whole effect was adorable. For all her resistance to filming before my arrival, she definitely seemed to have gotten camera-ready.

I knelt down to her, and we pressed our foreheads together. As I wheeled her to her room, past the silent faces that had kept me up all night, she told me about the night she'd had, listening to her portable radio.

"I can't sleep most nights," she said. "Nights are the loneliest time, awful. I just hold my stuffed cats an' listen to whatever staticky station I can pick up way out here."

Again I was at a loss as to how to assuage such loneliness. All I could say was "I'm sorry your night was so uncomfortable, Grandma. We're going to have fun today, okay?"

I wheeled her into her spot for filming and set up as casually as I could. Yesterday had gone so smoothly that I was superstitious about the second day. She just sat and waited for me to begin. And away we went.

Lucy: Okay, Grandma, yesterday we talked a lot about your young life. Today I'm going to ask more

about your mid-life. Where have you traveled in the
world?

Wanda: Oh, my gosh, with your father, the celebrity
life. We went to lots an' lots of places on concerts with
the Eagles.

I thought Wanda's matter-of-fact answer meant that
she had somehow gone off with my dad's band, the
Eagles, on a few international tours or something. I later
found out that Wanda only ever went to a single Eagles
show, and it was in Chicago while my parents were
dating, about 1975. She and Dale got to stand on the side
of the stage next to my dad's row of guitars, which is an
incredibly exciting place to be, with all the commotion
of switching out instruments between songs. For years
to come, my mom says, my grandparents particularly
spoke of the sea of light from the thousands of lighters
held in the air during "Hotel California."

Wanda had lived a life so totally apart from the world
of rock-and-roll, she had not had an inkling what it was
all about. Meeting a celebrity, let alone having one in
the family, brought incredible excitement to my mom's
relatives. I can see how this solitary VIP concert stood
out as a huge deal in Wanda's mind, stretching into an
imagined and embellished travel experience. Knowing
she attended just the one show, I find her answer so
sweet, so human—taking a singular experience and
retelling it on a much larger scale, as if it put her at the
center of the universe. It's a ridiculous and endearing
facet of being human. She told me about her brush with
celebrity life, as she called it, more than once.

My life, however, has very much unfolded in the world of celebrity, and that's given me a powerful perspective on what being human is, and what it is not. My first dozen years were spent within the normalcy of my mom and Jim Dad, far from the world of show business, and I only saw my dad a few times a year. He was still leading a tumultuous lifestyle, and it didn't mix well with children.

Though our visits were usually supervised, getting to see my dad always felt like Christmas day, but it couldn't erase the fact that unconsciously I was physically and emotionally guarded. I adored him, but I didn't trust him, and this shows up in photos of us then. I am always leaning away from him with my arms crossed over my body: a child's attempt at feeling safe in an insecure environment, nervous it could be ripped away again. He would leave without warning, that I knew for sure. So why should I love him at all, I remember thinking, if it just hurts again every time? It wasn't my dad's fault. He has always been on his own journey.

My mom gave me the gift of marrying an amazing man who became a stable father for me; but as I grew old enough to learn that my parents had broken up upon my arrival, I developed a devastating unspoken belief that it had been because of me. My child's heart decided that my father had abandoned my mom because I was not lovable, not good enough, not worthy; he simply didn't want me.

As if that fear wasn't destructive enough, I punished myself with another layer of shame: *You have a new dad, you ungrateful brat, it's more than a lot of kids have! Jim Dad loves you as his own and would no sooner abandon you than take his own life. How dare you pine for a man who didn't want you?*

And the cherry of self-torture atop that was feeling that even the thought of missing my first dad was a betrayal of Jim Dad. It's as if I was torn between two lovers, in love with both and paralyzed with guilt. These confusing feelings fragmented my young sense of self. As both my original parents went on to have children with new spouses, I secretly felt like an outsider. I was part of each new family unit, and I could peek in here and peek in there, but deep down I felt I didn't completely belong anywhere. As with all of us, I've always craved a sense of total belonging, and because I didn't know until very recently how to find that wholeness within myself, I searched for it in the people around me.

I had no idea my dad was famous until I was twelve years old. Before then, I saw him play a few club concerts, but nothing to speak of. Then life changed in two major ways—for him, for me, for our whole family. The first change was that my dad entered sobriety, for the first time. I remember standing in the kitchen hearing my mom on the phone with my dad's assistant, Smokey, who was telling her Joe was in a rehab facility and wanted to see me as soon as possible.

"Of course," she said. She'd always told my dad that as soon as he got straight, she would be there to make sure we had a relationship, and she honored her word. I was taken to his side, and I stayed with him a lot as he healed and reclaimed his life. His hair, which had always been long, brown, and scraggly, was now cut short and dyed platinum, and I remember being in a store with him, catching a glimpse of him from far away, and thinking with happiness, Who is this strange new person in my life? We really enjoyed getting to know each other, and in the years to come became incredibly close. My Jim Dad handled it beautifully, and I never needed to split my love again.

The second life-altering change was that the Eagles, who'd broken up in the seventies, reunited for the Hell Freezes Over tour when I was twelve, and I was taken to the VH1 taping of their first show, live on a soundstage at Sony Pictures. I sat between Whoopi Goldberg and Claudia Schiffer, both faces I recognized, and I began to suspect my dad was someone special.

Before my dad went onstage, performing sober for the first time pretty much ever, I wrote him a message on a napkin and put it on his dressing-room mirror: "Dear Dad—I'm so proud of you. And I love you lots!! Hope I see you on sunday." Amazingly, a cameraperson thought to capture it, and my little napkin note was featured in the *History of the Eagles* documentary. Check it out!

That was the night I realized he was famous, but there was a second night when I really got it. The Eagles were playing a sold-out Rose Bowl, in Pasadena, and from high up above the crowd in a box seat, I was shocked to tears when my dad came out onstage and a mass of 89,702 fans erupted into the loudest roar I had ever heard. Literally; tears were streaming down my face.

To tie that into these pages, what I've learned from

having a famous parent deeply influenced me to write about being human. I've witnessed a great divide between the flesh-and-blood dad of my heart and the celebrity guy that the public loves to spew dramatized Google facts about. It is truly all smoke-and-mirrors; at the end of the day, we all love and breathe and eat and laugh and cry and defecate the same. A Google search can tell us what people have achieved, but it can't tell us who they are. For that, we have to talk. We have to share our stories—all the vivid, messy, living details. Our hearts and lives are fathomless and intricate, no matter how outwardly simple or flashy they may appear.

Take Wanda—Wanda's life was not a grand one. After all, she didn't change the world with an invention or a discovery, she wasn't a political or business leader, she didn't contribute any works of art…hell, she barely even left her hometown. It is that way for countless lives, which seemingly fade in and out between birth and death with barely a blip on the radar. Yet each is equally valuable, and none is as uncomplicated as it may seem from the outside.

Wanda's life was plenty tempestuous.

Lucy: What did your parents think of Grandpa at first?

Wanda: Oh, my God, Mom loved Dale, an' Dad did, too. Yes, they really loved him, because they knew how the first one had did me an' remembered everythin' he did to hurt me. So therefore they, uh, turned to Dale when I started goin' with him. It was after I divorced Henry completely, although he brought a lawyer against me an' tried to prove that I was doin' this an' doin' that beforehand, before the divorce. But it didn't go over, an' we went on about our own business an' took care of ourself.

Lucy: So Henry was still coming around when you began dating Grandpa?

Wanda: Oh, sure, because we had our son together. Henry wasn't interested in bein' a dad, but he came around while Dale was there. Henry was a showoff, that's what it was, an' even though I had twice as much personality as Henry ever thought of havin', I just didn't throw it around like he did with his, I didn't throw it around, because it was not necessary. If people didn't like me an' what I stood for, they just didn't like me. They'd leave me alone, an' I'd leave them alone. Henry would pay attention to all that, an' I would say, "Well, you show off all the time, so I've got a right to show off with my few friends...take it or leave it, I don't care what you do."

Lucy: Did Henry tell you he was in love with you when he first came around visiting your parents?

Wanda: Oh, yeah, he told me he loved me, an' of course I know that he did. But it was the wrong way. He was a good guy, but he was a bad guy on the side... because he could not be true to no woman an' you couldn't tell what he was gonna do the next minute. Durin' our marriage, when I finally said, "This is it, Henry Ervin, I've had it...I can't go any farther," that was the day when he had tried to kill me. It happened in the kitchen of our tiny house, an' I remember thinkin', "Jesus, little Henry's in his crib in the front bedroom,

I've got to get him out!"

I managed to get the baby, an' that's when I filed suit for divorce. I said, "This has gone too far, I'm scared to death of him, an' we're not livin' with him anymore." He brought a lawyer against me, tried to fight the case… but he didn't get nowhere, because there was nowhere to get.

Lucy: Did you tell Grandpa Dale about those things when you were dating?

Wanda: Sure! Told him all about it. Had to, as Henry was still tryin' to come around an' mess me up.

Lucy: How did Dale propose to you?

Wanda: Oh, just "Let's get married!" That was the way it was. So we went to Tuscola, got married there. An' Dale's folks stood up with us, Clinton an' Marie Boyer. An' Reverend Kelly was our minister. Then he got killed, because he was shipped out in the service an' lost his life over in the foreign countries in the war, fightin' to help with the doctor situation. But before he got killed, he's the one that married us, Reverend Kelly.

Lucy: Do you remember your wedding dress?

Wanda: I wore a little, uh, striped royal blue an' white top, with a silk bottom dress. I didn't wear anythin' in my hair. We got married that day an' made life the way we wanted it.

Lucy: Did you go on a honeymoon?

Wanda: Well, we went out to his folks' farm after we got married, an' went to sleep in the big iron bed that you slept in last night over at Talor's house. For our honeymoon, that's what we wanted, an' that's what we did.

Lucy: Did you have a good time?

Wanda: Oh, yes, a wonderful time. In those days, you took it right on the chin, anythin' that turned up. You was tickled to death for it, you was just more than tickled. I was always all gratitude an' so was Dale. We was both made with gratitude stickin' out all over us, 'cause that's the way we wanted it.

Lucy: And where did you go with Grandpa in your first years, before you had children?

Wanda: We used to go, Dale an' I, up to Chicago once a year for a few days for the WLS Barn Dance Show....

The National Barn Dance, broadcast by WLS-AM in Chicago, Illinois, from 1924 to 1960, was one of the first American country-music radio programs, a direct precursor of the Grand Ole Opry.

Wanda: Then we went to Colorado umpteen times, because Dale had a brother an' his wife lived out in Colorado, he married a Colorado girl. We danced to Lawrence Welk in Elitch Gardens out in Colorado. I had a good time everywhere I went, 'cause that's the way I'm made.

Lucy: Did you ever go to Europe?

Wanda: Uh, I have been to Canada, the only foreign country, to see Niagara Falls. Dale wanted to take me over to England an' all those foreign countries before he got sick with Alzheimer's, but I said, "No, thanks." I refused to go, because I didn't lose anythin' over there in the war like he did, so I just took it as past-time talk on his part.

Lucy: Did you ever think about moving away from Illinois?

Wanda: Never thought about it at all, never thought about it. We had too many things right here in Illinois to be thinkin' about somethin' else, we didn't never think about things that we knew couldn't happen...an' so it just went on that way.

Lucy: And then you had your first daughter, Susie.

Wanda: We was married in '40, an' Susie was born in '42, right before Dale shipped off to war. We had Susie an' little Henry. Then we didn't have any more children for a long time, an' I worked for my livin', as well as Dale did. He opened the Legion in Urbana, an' I helped him with everythin' I could. We worked together an' enjoyed life as much as we could. That was before the war.

When Wanda refers to the Legion in Urbana, she's talking about the nation's largest veterans-service organization, the American Legion. Created by a group of officers who served in the American Expeditionary Forces in France during World War I, it was a hopeful idea for improving troop morale. It took off when it was officially chartered by Congress in 1919, and throughout World War II and into the modern age of continued wars, American Legions have been a social staple of almost every town in the country. In 1942, just before my grandfather was sent to fight, he helped with the operational details of opening the first American Legion in Urbana, Post 71.

Wanda: About eight years after the war finished an' Dale came home again, I began to have some female aggravations. So I went to the doctor, an' they said,

"Well, you got to be operated on." An' surprisingly, they said I was pregnant for Kathy, after eight years of no children. They said, "You'll have to be operated on before havin' this baby." So I went ahead with the operation, an' then I had Kathy. I think that's what slowed her down, the operation an' the drugs. She just wasn't up to par when it came to her IQ an' a few other things that was outstanding that she shoulda been adjusted in but couldn't have been. She just never could catch up. An' then seventeen months later, I had your mama Jody.

Lucy: Did you plan my mom?

Wanda: Well, no, I didn't, an' then I told Dale to stay away from me, because he was full of babies. He just laughed an' looked at me an' said, "My, my, my, where was you all that time?" I said, "Well, I was right there, naturally!" But anyway, I wasn't too happy, because I went too many years between each child, too many years.

Lucy: You just didn't want any more kids?

Wanda: Yeah, that's the way I was, that's the way I felt. Your mama Jody came along an' she was just as sharp as, uh, well, you know how sharp she is. She was always happy an' good-natured an' everythin' that went with it. I had to live my life over again because of havin' a second family. Well, actually a third family. But it turned out real good, except that little Kathy was hindered with slowness an' her IQ was below normal.

Lucy: How old was she when you noticed she was developing slower?

Wanda: Well, she didn't, uh, talk until she was three years old. An' we noticed it then because our other children, Henry Ervin an' Susan, had been so up an' comin', ya know—alert by the same time. So, all the time it was touch an' go with Kathy. We always sent her to special-education schooling.

Lucy: Did you take her to a doctor?

Wanda: Yes, we did. They said her, uh, mentality was due to the fact that I had surgery…which meant quite a bit, because it was pretty serious to even give birth to her. So they blamed it mostly on that. I didn't realize at the time that little Kathy was the way she was. God bless her heart, she's the best little girl that ever thought of bein'. She can't help it, she's just born that way an' that's the way she's always lived.

Lucy: From pictures I've seen of my mom and Kathy, they were the best of friends.

Wanda: Oh, they were little dolls! Just absolutely dolls!

Lucy: And I think my mom took care of Kathy and protected her.

Wanda: Oh, yeah.

Lucy: What did you love most about being a mother?

Wanda: Well, I think I loved bein' a mother because it was born an' bred right in me, the same as my own mother havin' twelve children. I didn't want that many, an' I didn't have that many. I had five children. I love my kids, I love 'em dearly, and I've always loved 'em, always will.

CHAPTER TEN

I WAS READY TO ask her about her husband being sent away to the war with Hitler, and I thought maybe bringing out his letters would inspire more memories.

"So," I said, "I have some of Grandpa's letters to share with you."

Her mouth fell open as I pulled out my tin box with the sixty-three letters. She lightly brushed her hand back and forth across the yellowed envelopes and didn't speak for a long moment.

Forty-two of the letters are handwritten, and twenty-one are V-mail, or "Victory Mail." V-mail was developed to help the military handle and expedite the overwhelming amount of mail being sent back and forth between the troops and their families. It worked like this: A soldier would write a letter on a special form that would be photographed on a smaller scale in microfilm. The reels of microfilm were flown back home, reprinted, and delivered to the recipients. In a nutshell, a photocopy, shrunk down to about half-size. Since the number of letters was in the multibillions per year, this V-mail method greatly furthered the war effort by drastically freeing up tons of shipping and airplane space needed for valuable supplies.

What makes having these twenty-one V-mails of my grandfather's extra special is that more than one billion were processed between 1942 and 1945. Then they disappeared forever. This makes mine part of a limited edition.

"And here are your portraits," I said, pulling out sepia sweetheart photos of her and Dale in their joined frame of green and gold. She held them up close to her eyes.

"Oh, my GOSH, I remember that real well. Isn't that somethin'! God bless his soul."

Lucy: I'd like to hear how it was for you when Grandpa went away to the war. How was that for you?

Wanda: Well, it was a very lonely atmosphere everywhere. But I had to make the best of it, because of my children. See, when Dale went in, it was '43, we'd been married not even three years.

I pulled a letter at random from the box and opened it. "This letter right here says February 2, 1945, so two years into him being away. He ends every single letter the same," I ran my finger down the page, "'With all my love and kisses, your husband.'"

Wanda smiled her four-toothed grin. "Yeah, that was Dale, through and through. He always did that, always did."

Lucy: So tell me about when you would get his letters.

Wanda: Well, the mail came right to our front door. I would read his letter an' then I would sit down an' write him back. Then I would walk up to the post office near Lincoln Square, an' I would have my cryin' spell, missin' him like crazy. I would go up there an' mail him out a letter to relieve my soul an' my body an' my love for my husband. That's the only thing I had to live on, his letters an' my children.

I tried to make the best of my life before me, an' he didn't get home until '45...1945, after the whole war had taken place. They took him from me when Susan was only eight months old, an' Henry Ervin wasn't much more than four years old. So he left two babies an' me, alone. I did all the grocery buyin', bill payin', everythin', because Uncle Sam said, "You have got to go." They drafted 'em married or unmarried during World War Two, just drafted 'em, swiped right out from under ya. You had no say-so about what they did, they just did it.

Lucy: Do you remember the day he came home?

Wanda: It was a reunion that you never forget. It had its good points, but it had its unforgivin' an' unforgotten points, too.

Lucy: Was he different when he came home?

Wanda: He didn't seem to be, but I know he didn't speak of the things he saw an' done, he just couldn't. Most men went crazy with it, he just got real quiet. He never changed too much, he was just Dale.

Lucy: Were you ever with another man while he was away?

Wanda: I would go to town once every week or two with my sister. An' I didn't ever drink beer at that time at all. I drank a mixed drink of, oh, I don't even remember what I did drink, it was a mixed drink of some kind. I would get my sister who lived next door to take care of the children, because I had to have someone watch 'em, they couldn't be alone. An' then I would go up to the Embassy Tavern an' the Rose Bowl to hear the music with my other sister, an' we'd have a drink or two, an' then she'd bring me home, 'cause she had a car an' I didn't even have a car.

One night there was a soldier there at the tavern, an' he got to talkin' to me, which you can do easy enough. He was stationed up at Chanute Field by Rantoul, he got down on a bus, I s'pose. An' he said, "How about me walkin' you home?" An' I said, "Well, you can walk me home, but that's it." Well, when we got to my house, he just barged hisself right in the door. I had a heatin' stove in the dinin' room at that time…. I thought, "Boy, oh boy, you're sure a brave one. I told you I was a married woman an' I was true to my husband." And he just…I had a heck of a time with him. That's the only one I had anyways near a sexual life with. No way, no way, couldn't possibly. Then I felt badly, because I was still goin' up to the tavern to hear the music, an' I started thinkin', "I don't need to be doin' this, it leads to no good." So I just quit doin' it.

Lucy: And what about Grandpa Dale; did he have any kind of affair when he was in the war?

Wanda: Well, I don't know what he done for sure. I don't think so.

Lucy: In his letters, he says things like, "I'm saving all my love for you, honey." "All the guys are drinking but I don't want to drink, because it leads to no good." "I don't think I'm going to go into Paris, because you know where that can lead." Things like that.

Wanda: Yep. All the girls went for the GIs, just like nobody's business. They just went for 'em, went for 'em. So you know, when I'd get a letter from him, I'd say, "Well, he's a good one if he can keep away from them females over there." I always made a jokin' rule of it, you know, made a joke of it, because I had to. But I'm pretty assured he was faithful all the time he was in the service. He didn't have to be but just was, I think.

Lucy: Did you talk to him on the phone at all, or was it just the letters?

Wanda: Nope, nope, just strictly letters...I was in Urbana an' he was in France, the U.K., wherever the war took him. I'll never forget gettin' my letters from him, an' walkin' up to the post office to mail him back. The letters took weeks an' weeks, sometimes months, to reach us back an' forth, but we didn't care, we just kept sendin' 'em. That's why sometimes you'd send two or three in a day, you was just wantin' to talk to the other one so desperately. None of the letters I wrote survived the war, naturally, Dale couldn't keep 'em over there for savin'.

Lucy: What type of work did Grandpa do in the war?

Wanda: He went into office work, he didn't have to be on the front line, like his brother Don was. So that was a good thing. But he was among all the frontline fightin'. He said when he landed in Normandy by boat the day after it happened, there were dead sailors in the water an' floatin' around everywhere, so many bodies they couldn't walk without steppin' on top of 'em. I said that was enough. He never talked anymore about the service.

But that man named George sittin' at our table at lunch, he talks about the service now an' then, now an' then. He's always got to bring some kind of gruesome story into the act, but I don't care to hear it, I don't care to hear it at all. 'Cause what I don't know don't hurt me. But what I do know hurts me very bad. That's the way life is, especially my life.

Lucy: Did you have friends die in the war?

Wanda: Oh, my heavens, yes. A whole bunch of 'em. Sure, that was one of them things. But you learned to take care of everythin' in hand an', uh, take care of your own life, what you had to do to live.

An' here I am, still here, an' Dale's gone. You don't understand a lot of this yet, you don't understand, because it's just one of those things that is piled down on your soul an' your body when you're old. I keep thinkin'…he's where he's at in heaven, an' I'm still down here, an' I cry every night. An' I think about all you children, an' I think about this, an' I think about that, but what good does it do?

I miss my home in Urbana that I lived in since Dale an' I was first married. We had it made over an' worked over—had a big dinin' room built onto the kitchen, carport made, an' front porch all glassed in. We had that perfect home, an' my neighbors came over to see me constantly. A young couple bought it now. People say they've redone it again since we had it, they say I wouldn't recognize the place now. I said, "What do you mean I wouldn't know it? I would too know it, I would know it for as long as I lived there"…which was some seventy years.

Lucy: How long were you married?

Wanda: We was married sixty-four years when I brought him down here with the Alzheimer's.

Lucy: Tell me about that; how was it for you when

Grandpa got sick?

Wanda: I heard that Dale had an affair with some…
bitch in Urbana. An' I'm pretty sure I figured out who
it is, I'm pretty sure I have. I'm surmisin' the woman
that mighta had the affair an' how long it took place,
two an' a half years. I'm just surmisin', I'm just guessin'
—guesswork, you see? An' then he went right into
Alzheimer's, because of how he did what he did. I think
it was self-punishment; the brain couldn't stand the
punishment so it left his body. I cry about that.

Lucy: Did you ever ask him about it?

Wanda: Well, by the time I heard, he had already
developed the Alzheimer's, so it was too late. He was
gradually startin' downhill. He couldn't remember
what was happenin', that's the way Alzheimer's does
you. He'd overtaxed his brain, if he had indeed had
that affair. You put everythin' together, an' you have
to wonder exactly how "Oldtimer's" takes place with
three-quarters of the people in this world. What happens to make it start? Is there actually somethin' that
does make it start, or is it just old age creepin' up day by
day an' night by night? You think about all that, every
square inch of you thinks.

Lucy: I remember being at your house when Grandpa
was still at home; I remember him looking out the front
door saying his mom was out there. Did he do things
like that a lot?

Wanda: Well, he would say different things to you
that would prove his mentality was slippin' pretty
fast. He'd wander off out in front an' stand there in the
driveway at the entrance to our home. Just stand there

an' look out an' look an' look an' look—you could see his head turnin' back an' forth.

I'd say, "Kathy, go out there an' get your father. Because he's standin' out there in the driveway an' you never know when he's goin' to take more steps in the wrong direction." So she'd go right out an' bring her dad in, if she could. A lot of times he'd say, "No, I'm not movin'!" an' there was nothin' we could do to help him come back to this reality.

Lucy: Did he try to sleep with you, try to be sexual, after he got Alzheimer's?

Wanda: Not much, although he did go for me a few times near the end…he'd start gettin' riled, an' I'd say, "Don't start what you can't finish!" He thought he was twenty years old again!

But we never had no sexual life for twelve or fifteen years before that, we never had it. That's why I think that he did have another woman. Women. He worked around 'em constantly, an' them Boyers' sexual resistance was never too strong, none of 'em. His dad's sexual resistance, his brothers', none of 'em.

While Wanda thinks her husband's Alzheimer's came from his guilt over cheating poisoning his brain, she's overlooking the fact that he wasn't the first in his family to develop the disease. (Not to mention the science.) Dale began his struggle with Alzheimer's in his early eighties, and by the time he passed away, at eighty-nine, it had taken him pretty completely.

My mom swears he recognized his wife and kids until the very end, but who really knows? I do know that at the end he couldn't differentiate us grandkids from a hole in the wall. He would stare at us in bewilderment and politely call us "sweetie." I got the feeling he was wondering who these strange children in his house were, and when we would be leaving.

When we visited during those years, we began to see sides of him that were alien to us, and it was frightening. While always soft-spoken and quiet, he became completely silent, his mouth tightly shut, a scowl on his face and monstrous desperate fear in his eyes. That's what scared me most, those eyes. They became filled with a frenzy of emotions, or lack of: glazed and vacant, stone-cold anger, confusion, fury, back to glazed. He looked like a scared child who was panicking but not sure who to ask for help. He was sinking into his body, unable to call out, and all we could do was watch.

Many people who lose someone to this disease describe the same helplessness. Just as he couldn't come to us for comfort, we couldn't go to him. There was no way to talk about it. Now when we stayed with my grandparents, their once joyous and lively home was quiet and tense.

Just as I had always observed Dale's behavior, I observed him as he disappeared. He sat in the armchair where he had sipped his beer, but now he had no beer. Now he sat with his hands folded in his lap like a boy in a waiting room. He stared straight ahead, his pale blue eyes watering, blinking, waiting. He took to wearing the same brown button-up, collared shirt every single day; it had to be wrestled away from him every so often for a wash. I never knew if it was because he liked it so much or because he didn't know he was choosing the same shirt on repeat.

After he died, I took it home. I'd style it with tight black pants, make it fashionable, feel close to Dale when I wore it. But when my brother said it would mean a lot to him to have it, I knew the shirt had chosen him instead of me. Spencer has proven to be the rightful protector of that particular heirloom, and I have to say, no shirt has ever earned its retirement more.

One night during the seven long years of Dale's demise, we were all having dinner at the kitchen table: my mom, Jim Dad, my siblings, Dale, Wanda, Aunt Kathy, and me. Fried bologna, collard greens, and rhubarb pie were on the menu. I hadn't touched my food, since Kathy had for sure nibbled on it in the fridge. My mom tried to engage Grandpa in conversation about an old colleague at the university, where he had worked in administration for thirty-five years. Ignoring her repeated questions, he slowly stood up, walked to the stove, and turned all four burners on to high flame.

We sat watching this disturbing scene in confusion. My grandmother broke the silence and scolded him loudly. "Dale, quit that an' come back to the table!"

He just watched the fires with a forlorn look in his eyes.

The next night, we had finished another defiled dinner, some type of fried meat and collard greens, and were sitting around the living room when Dale got up and headed to the front door as if something was bothering him. The door had three staggered panes of vertical rectangular glass, and he stood before them with his arms at his sides, anxiously looking out into the dark, snowy night.

When Wanda yelled at him to get away from the door, he snapped at her. "I gotta get ready for Mom, she's out there waitin' for me."

His mom, my Great-Grandma Marie, had been dead for ten years. And yet, because he was so certain, I was convinced he was seeing her ghost. I felt he knew *exactly* what he was talking about, and we were the crazy ones. Terrified that Marie's ghost would knock at any second, I worriedly glanced back and forth at the adults.

Wanda had no patience for this and barked, "Come back an' relax in your chair! Your mother's dead an' gone a long time now, Dale!"

He stayed glued to that door, his blue eyes blinking away tears. I know that Wanda's anger was because she was afraid, but I'm not sure this was the best way to handle him. Being told he was wrong wasn't going to get him out of whatever reality he was stuck in.

Of course, we all handle fear differently. Some of us yell and scold; others laugh and joke. Some go loud, some go quiet, take charge, give up. Wanda's fear made her lash out like a stern parent. I was afraid for Grandpa, too, but I felt unable to help, so my fear turned me into a numb onlooker. Filthy liar that it is, Fear tells me I am insignificant, that I don't understand what I'm experiencing, and so I have to fight the overwhelming urge to disassociate. What lie does Fear tell you?

Over the coming months, Dale's Alzheimer's became more and more difficult for Wanda to handle. The physical incidents were more frequent. One night as she struggled to get him into the shower, he pushed her so hard, she fell, and her leg was cut and bleeding. The truth everyone had been avoiding was impossible to deny, and Dale was moved out of the house he had called home for sixty-four years.

Once mandated to his new life at the nursing home, he was more lost than ever behind those angry, glazed eyes. He was usually placed in a wheelchair by a window, his hands folded in his lap. For years, Wanda visited him faithfully once a week, until he was taken to the hospital with organ failure and passed away before sunrise on a Sunday morning in January. Although he had been in the hospital for several days, she chose not to visit him there.

I wondered (judged) at the time, *How could a wife not want to stay by her husband's side until his last breath?* But Wanda had said something very revealing when she talked to me about Dale's wartime experiences. She said, "What I don't know can't hurt me, but what I do know hurts me very much." Dale's actual death was not something she could face, and so she avoided those final hours.

I must respect Wanda's emotional limits, and everyone's, really, for I've turned away from far less trauma than that myself. What I regret most is that I turned from my mom as she went through a painful divorce from my Jim Dad in 2010.

For a whole decade before they separated, their marriage had been a challenge for both of them, and though they tried to keep their unhappiness from my siblings and me, we could feel it. We didn't know what "it" was, just that there was no warmth between them.

As I moved to Hollywood and began my music career at twenty-one, my mom and Jim Dad moved with Grace and Spencer, then sixteen and fourteen, to Pennsylvania for Jim Dad's work. Looking back, I think that being left behind was more traumatizing for me than I realized; perhaps beginning to tour immediately after they left reflected that. I actually got to see them often, in and around Pennsylvania. Although that overjoyed me and we had great times, I could tell they weren't doing well.

Within five years, my Jim Dad was back in L.A. and living with me, while my mom stayed on in PA so that Grace and Spencer could have the stability of finishing high school and entering college there. Our parents were officially divorcing. Each had their reasons, and good ones, too. The thing about kids in a divorce, though, adult kids included, is that they typically can't help but feel the need to take a side. I became Jim Dad's protector, reasoning that my mom had my siblings with her and Jim Dad only had me. I didn't know the depth of my mom's pain, so I fearfully, and unconsciously, shut her out. Then Fear used its buddy, Judgment, to justify itself, and so I blamed her.

After a time, I felt an overwhelming false responsibility to fix this for both of them, though there wasn't a thing I could do. I hated their pain even more, wanted it as far from me as possible, and Fear's response was to cast them both out until it passed. So I shut Jim Dad out, too, telling him he couldn't live with me anymore. The divorce was no one's fault, of course, and if I had been more emotionally mature, I would've known that all I had to do was to love them. All they needed (like every one of us) was to be told that everything would be okay. At twenty-six, I just didn't have the tools yet. Like Wanda, I avoided those final hours.

CHAPTER ELEVEN

WITH ALL THIS TALK of my grandfather's cheating and getting Alzheimer's, Wanda had become quite agitated, so I decided to end the interview for the day. To lift her spirits, I took her on a stroll down to the glassed-in patio. I wheeled her down the halls so she could say hello to everyone and give her opinions about everything.

"That's George, he took Meredith's little sister to the senior dance," she whisper-yell repeated as we passed him in his wheelchair. George must've been a stallion in his day; he had obviously made quite an impression on the women.

I left her that second day with our forehead press, telling her to rest up, because we would be continuing our talk one final time tomorrow.

This work was emotionally draining for both of us, but it was still early in the day, and I had a lot to document while it was daylight. After learning about my grandparents' honeymoon night in that iron bed at the Boyer family farm (which, after seeing Wanda recall it with such a devious glint in her eye, I was now grossed out about sleeping in), I couldn't wait to get out to the farm and photograph it.

I picked up Cousin Talor on the way, giving her no choice, really, as I needed her to find the place. She got behind the wheel, and as she expertly drove the open, unmarked roads, I held my camera out the window and recorded footage of the landscape, which I was of course collecting for my future-film ideas.

As we rounded a wooded patch of road, Dale's parents' old farmhouse came into view, and I cried out. It was a magical sight, and waves of nostalgia flooded my mind. The Boyer family home is a two-story house with two front windows downstairs, an upstairs dormer window, and a wide, banistered front porch. The bottom half of the house had been painted a deep red, and the roof, forest green. By the time I came onto the scene in the eighties, the color had faded, and the effect was charming. By this winter day in 2011, the house had been painted white. The front of the house gazes out at the road, and I could see the very room on the second floor where Dale and Wanda had spent their wedding night.

As I had done at Wanda's family farm the day before, we parked across the road so as not to alarm anyone. Talor suggested we politely stand by the car and enjoy our memories, but I had every intention of asking to go inside. As soon as we approached the front gate, the farm dog came to the fence and began wildly barking, alerting his owner, who was working in one of the barns. The man set down his work, and waved as he started out toward us. He had no idea who these people on his property were, but still, he was kind and welcoming from the first glance. *Wow, Illinois really is magical.*

There were tall trees, mostly hickory, all around the house. Those hickory trees have been on the Boyer farm for well over a hundred years and are very special to my family. When Wanda and Dale married and bought their house in town, they brought hickory seeds, as well as saplings of maple and red bud, from the farm to plant in their front yard. Many of the Boyer siblings did the same with various trees at their new homes. Even now on my bookshelf, I have three hickory nuts from the farm sitting next to a picture of my husband, Will, and me on the farm steps—the same spot where Wanda and Dale posed for pictures in 1940 on their wedding day.

As Talor and I reached the brick path to the porch, I marveled at it: Dale's brother Beryl had laid the bricks, each stamped with a special Boyer mark, by hand. When my grandparents bought their little house, Dale took some of these original bricks for their walkway.

One hundred years on, the bricks were very uneven. We stepped carefully onto the first step to the porch, the heart of the Boyer family home, where practically every important occasion had been photographed. I thought again of how once-special places, where so much life has occurred, just fade away when the people who made them special are gone.

The owner met us on the porch, apologizing for the sweaty mess he was from his chores, and introduced himself as Rich. We in turn apologized for disturbing him and explained who we were—that our great-grandparents had been the Boyers who built the house, and it had meant a lot to us growing up, yada yada. I sheepishly asked if we could come inside the house for a moment.

Of course it was no problem, and Rich warmly invited us in, although he never left us alone at any point. I didn't blame him. He and his family had bought the place around 1990 and raised their kids there; another cycle of life on this spot, *dust to dust*. As we crossed the threshold, it was like going back in time. Quiet, dark, as if the wood-paneled rooms soaked up all the outside sound and sunlight.

Living room, archway to dining room, staircase built into the back corner, bedroom off to the right—these rooms were original but larger now, remodeled for this new family's comfort. They had expanded a "summer kitchen" at the back of the house as well; it was now porched in and lovely. Upstairs were three more original bedrooms, which I forced myself not to ask to see. Even with the home's expansions, much of the original dark-wood detail was still visible and beautiful. The house had been fashioned with hand-hewn beams, cut from trees on the property, which you could see in door frames, closets, the staircase, and in the attic.

I slowly walked from room to room over the worn wooden floorboards; slanted at odd angles here and there, they creaked under my feet. When we weren't conversing with Rich, the ticking of the grandfather clock at the foot of the stairs echoed in the stillness. I smelled the damp, the dust, very old things—like the smell of a hundred-year-old book when you fan its pages under your nose—mingled with the aromas of food cooking.

I shivered, passing through cold spots in these dark rooms where my long-ago family members had spent their hours. Now this new family's keepsakes—crocheted quilts, needlepoint pillows, books, framed photographs—had replaced ours. *How did you decorate these rooms, Great-Grandma Marie?* Perhaps the same

155

way she decorated the rooms of the dollhouse where we had our peaches.

We stepped out the back door of the summer kitchen to see the grounds, and Rich stayed walking and talking with us as we explored: the beautiful old barns our family had built, even an original outhouse, complete with toilet paper and reading material—unnecessary now, though someone obviously preferred it in a pinch. Talor laughed at me as I photographed it.

Outbuildings, chicken coops, and barns dotted the grassy land, and back behind the house, a hill rolled down to a fence with a beautiful gate. My mom recalls that a heavy old iron propped that gate open when she was a child. Beyond the gate was a lazy creek, a large pasture, and then the dense woods. My mom had her very own hill in that wood, named for her by Dale. Father and daughter spent many hours together, walking on Jody's Hill. I remember walking there as a child, thinking my mom must be someone incredibly important to have her own hill.

That night back at Talor and Tim's, Aunt Kathy joined us for dinner. Talor had driven her from her group home, as she often did so that Kathy could have plenty of family time. I gave my aunt a longer hug than usual. I felt closer to her after talking with Wanda, although she'd never know that. Kathy was her jovial, childlike self. She immediately asked if I had brought her a present, which I realized I had not. I quickly thought of something.

"Aunt Kathy, I have something very special for you; here, I keep it in my coin purse."

As I pulled out my bag, she asked me if it was money.

"Even better!" I said and gave her a small amber crystal I kept with me for luck and protection. "This is a very special crystal, it will bring you good luck wherever you go."

She grabbed the crystal, quickly put it in her pocket without really looking at it, and exclaimed, "Thank you, Lucy, wow, thank you!"

We sat at the table for a long time and laughed into the night. Somehow we all had a shorthand that connected us, no matter how much time went by between visits. I still had another batch of Dale's letters to transcribe, so after kisses and hugs and extras for Aunt Kathy, I retreated to the iron love bed and spent another restless night in an army barracks outside Paris.

CHAPTER TWELVE

FOR THE THIRD MORNING in a row, Wanda was waiting for me on the bench by the nurses' station. She was pristine in white and teal today. She was very cheerful this morning, and as I knelt and we put our foreheads together, she pinched my nose and laughed. I had some surprises in store for Miss Wanda Mae today. I'd decided we would take a field trip, anywhere she wanted to go. I wanted to get her out of these sterile rooms and out into the world she knew and loved.

But first, I wanted to film her singing and playing the piano for me. As the nurses transferred Wanda from the bench to her wheelchair for our hallway journey, I mindlessly gazed into the dining room, where the usual suspects were taking in the morning. I flinched as I realized where my gaze had wandered, but was pleasantly surprised to see some lovely moments: four ladies talking at a table, doing a puzzle together, and a man in a wheelchair wheeling himself to the window and opening the blinds to look out. Wanda pulled my attention from the scene by beginning to introduce me yet again to the same people down the hall that I'd met the previous two days.

When we got to her room, I set her up at her electric keyboard. She proceeded to play and sing old gospel hymns for an hour, with her own spicy twist, of course. The ice orderly lumbered in and out, the alarm incessantly pinged in the hall, but the sunlight streaming through the window was stronger today, and Wanda's joyful music drowned out all the nursing-home annoyances.

Her fingers were so crooked, it amazed me she could hit the right notes. "The trick is," she said without stopping, "that I aim for one key over from the one I'm tryin' to play, so the fingertips end up where the song needs 'em to be."

She could play endlessly, songs she knew by heart. Her repertoire was immense; she could recall the chords and words to pop hits and church hymns alike. Many of the songs Wanda held in her brain are no longer in print; they can be found only in the dusty, century-old hymnals she learned from as a kid. She knew those hymnals practically cover to cover.

I have collected many of these tattered and faded songbooks from hole-in-the-wall shops around the world. As a child, I developed a perfect ear for pitch and harmony from singing gospel hymns with Wanda from these books, just as she had learned from her parents and practiced with her siblings. My mom would take a third part, and together we would harmonize and praise the Lord in song. I had no personal connection to Wanda's Christianity, but I adored singing the songs.

The last time the three of us sang together, it was "My Happiness" in Cousin Talor's living room. The song was one of Wanda's favorites, written (with different lyrics) by Borney Bergantine in 1933, when she was twenty, and later made popular with new generations by the 1959 Connie Francis Top 40 version.

Whether skies are gray or blue
Any place on earth will do
Just as long as I'm with you,
my happiness

Wanda sat in an armchair, with my mom and me at her feet, wailing the melody while my mom and I took the harmonies. (I recorded it with my phone, and if you'd like to hear us, you can find it on YouTube by typing in "MY HAPPINESS, REMEMBER ME AS HUMAN.")

Now, in the nursing home as she played, I continued asking her questions.

Lucy: Who taught you to play the piano?

Wanda: My mom. She could play anythin' by ear, just like I do, an' just like you do, it's a family trait. She'd just get the simple tune an' go from there. We had a piano, it was called a Jesse French. It was a very hard-hittin' piano, you couldn't hardly get the music out of it, but anyway, I learned on it. She taught me to sing beautiful, too, me an' Harold, until he was killed at school…we had the best singin' lessons with Mom.

Lucy: Can you play "Tiptoe Through the Tulips"? Will you play that for me?

Wanda: Oh, yeah….

It was on the tip of her fingers, and she immediately began….

Tiptoe through the window
By the window, that is where I'll be
Come tiptoe through the tulips with me

How different those nights of singing and laughing with her beloved Harold in their attic bed were from her nights now: long hours of radio static on her headphones; missing friends and family, almost all passed over now; neighbors dying in their beds, and only her stuffed cats to hold. Old age is not easy, I thought for the millionth time.

As she finished the song, a nurse walked by and clapped with enthusiasm. Wanda didn't notice but continued answering a question I hadn't even asked. She was reverting back to a young girl before my eyes.

Wanda: I was always a wiry little girl. Mommy an' I was close as close can be. I loved every part of my mother an' she loved me, an' she also loved all my children, every one of you.

Great-Grandma Nellie died before I was born, but Wanda looked so proud as she said this that I didn't correct her.

Lucy: Did your mom like jokes?
Wanda: Oooohhhh, my gosh, anythin' had fun to it an' laughs, she would just get the biggest kick out of it. Laughed just like a little girl about fifteen or sixteen years old instead of the age she was.
Lucy: Who taught you to love jokes in your life?
Wanda: Well, I think more or less I got it growin' up around my brothers. My dad would go to town to play Euchre with some fellas, an' he'd hear a joke or two, an' he'd come home an' tell it to all us kids. Of course, he'd be half full of liquor, an' he'd open up an' reeeeeallly

REMEMBER ME AS HUMAN

tell the jokes. Mom would sit around an' listen with us, then first thing you know, Mom would be tellin' 'em, too. An' they just went back an' forth, back an' forth between us all…then it would all cool off as quick as it had came on, the laughter. We was always very grateful for any fun or laughter, all my family was that way. My brothers an' sisters was all very…oooooh, outgoin'. My mother an' father could act out jokes left an' right.

Lucy: Can you tell me a joke?

Wanda: Oh, sure, oh, sure. There's the one about two women, two friends…one lives in a nice home out in the country, the other one come to visit her. So they were sittin' on the front porch in rockin' chairs…an' between the two rockin' chairs, there was a fresh-baked pie. An' so they just rocked back an' forth. "Oh, have you heard the latest about so-an'-so?" an' "You know what the weather's gonna be?" Pretty soon the visiting woman looked down at her friend's feet, an' noticed that there was her panties—clear down around her ankles. She says, "My goodness gracious, why, snakes alive, what you got your panties clear down around your ankles for?" An' the other one, you know what her reply was? "That's to keep the flies off of our pie!"

She stared at me with a wicked grin, enjoying my reaction.

Lucy: Wow, Grandma, you are a sick one.

Wanda: I thought that was kinda clever.

She was giggling like a mischievous kid, her mouth wide open, revealing her four remaining bottom teeth.

The sight made me laugh more than the actual joke.

Wanda: Then there was the one about the guy that was takin' a walk, this is another one. He was out takin' a walk early in the mornin'…an' he had to walk by a nursin' home. Out in front of the nursin' home was six middle-aged naked women, all rowed up, rowed up, out in the yard of the nursin' home. "My goodness gracious," he said. "If them women are still out on that lawn when I come back from my walk, I'm goin' to report 'em." So here he comes, traipsing back from his walk, an' there laid all six girls…all six of 'em still spread out naked. He rushed in, got ahold of the administrator. "Sir, you know you have six naked women out in your front yard?!" The administrator said, "Yes, sir, I do know about it, they are six…."

She paused and frowned, trying to remember what came next.

"Oh, what do you call a bad woman?" she asked me as she scratched her chin.

Lucy: A hussy?
Wanda: No, no, no, you call 'em by name…six, uh… oh, that's the whole punch line…there are six, uh… ohhhhhhhh, that ruins the whole joke.
Lucy: You'll remember it.
Wanda: Huh?
Lucy: You'll remember it in a minute…. Prostitutes?
Wanda: PROSTITUTES!!

She jumped forward in her wheelchair and triumphantly pointed her spindly finger at me.

Wanda: "They are six PROSTITUTES, an' they're all waitin' for today's yard sale to begin!"

She let the punch line ring out, then sat back with total satisfaction at the achievement of having finally remembered her joke. She kept grinning and mumbling under her breath, "That was the answer… six prostitutes…no wonder I never could remember that word…it's kind of a…different one."
When she finally recovered herself, I went on.

Lucy: So why do you think jokes are so important in life?
Wanda: Well, I used to go to parties quite a bit….
Lucy: No, not you!
Wanda: Uh huh, yeah, I did. They always would say, "Oh, we've got to ask Wanda to come, because she's the life of the party with her jokes." So I would go, an' before the evenin' was over, why, I'd liven things up, just tellin' my jokes. I would hear 'em here an' there, an' therefore I would tell 'em. I got a kick out of doin' 'em. Everyone got so that they would automatically ask me to the parties to delve in fun an' laughter, which I did. I was always, well…kind of "personality plus," that's what I was.

It all went together an' made a big beautiful party in the long run. Because life is supposed to be a big beautiful party in the long run. Jokes are very important, very. You have to know how to put forth a joke. If you don't know how, an' you clobber it up, or you mumble half of it, then you might as well just shut up. You have to be able to act 'em out, practically, there's no question about it, you just have to be able to do that with jokes. Just have to.

To Wanda, telling jokes was an art, and she was a connoisseur. We were on a positive high note, so it seemed a good time to head out on our field trip.

"Grandma, remember I said we would go on a drive today? It's time to go; where will it be?"

Without missing a beat, she said, "Dale's grave, naturally."

CHAPTER THIRTEEN

I HELPED HER FRESHEN her makeup and hair, finishing with a dab of her favorite perfume. My mom recalls that when she was young, Wanda wore a popular scent called Tweed. Wanda had switched to Wind Song, which I thought smelled like she'd bought it at the Dollar Store (no offense to Dollar Store shoppers), but she loved it.

After signing her out with the nurses, we were off and down the empty highway. Wanda couldn't see much of the world around her, but she knew exactly where she was. When I rolled the windows down a crack and let the cold winter air in, she closed her eyes and leaned into the wind.

At the cemetery, I parked the car and carefully helped Wanda out, supporting her as we walked to her husband's grave. Dale's plot held two more headstones, one with Wanda's name, the other with Kathy's. Their birthdates were already carved, but the rest was blank, to be inscribed with their death dates when their times came.

There it was, that familiar childhood pit of stress in my stomach at seeing graves, especially ones where my loved ones were headed. I kept my arm around Wanda as we stood before him, and even though she grimaced against the cold, I knew she was happy here with her love, looking and smelling beautiful for him. As happy as one could be, under the circumstances.

Hello again, Grandpa. I had not been here since he died, and thoughts of his burial day came crashing back. His funeral was held on January 7, just three days after his death. Because of an acting job, I couldn't join my family until the day of the funeral.

The night before, my mom called and asked me to speak for our family at Dale's service. *Twelve hours to come up with something to say; help.* I knew right away I wanted to make one of his war letters the central part of my speech, so I took all sixty-three with me and planned to use the flight time to choose the right one. I went to work before the plane took off, silently calling on my grandfather for help. *Okay, Grandpa, I have very little time to choose the right letter, so you show me which one you want.*

I read and waited for a lightning flash, and eventually I came to one letter, dated second to last in the collection, and was struck by all the emotions it held. This letter was sweet, playful, passionate, full of young love and bold hope. I laughed out loud at Dale's reserved but flirtatious sexual innuendos. This was the letter he wanted me to read; I knew it. And indeed, he gave me a sign of confirmation.

My mom was waiting for me when I landed, and as we drove to the funeral, I read her the letter. Halfway through...as I was reading the lines "I was very happy to receive four nice letters from you, written on the 8th of Jan. I think you must of had your dates mixed up a little, you were writing on Sun nite and Sun was the 7th. But that's OK just so long as you write"...my mom gasped.

"Lucy! He just said Grandma was mistaken and actually wrote him on January 7th...and *today* is January 7th!" There it was, Dale's chuckle at the letter he had chosen for me to read.

Grandpa's funeral was in the typical Midwest style of our family: open casket, hymn music played by the resident organist, people dressed in black filling the pews. Wanda was in the front row, her head lowered. She looked so fragile in her grief. I went to her and kissed her cheek. Her husband of sixty-four years was gone, and now she faced an alien life without him.

People milled past her, kissing her hands, whispering their regret as she noiselessly wept. And up in front, surrounded by a patriotic spray of white, red, and blue flowers, was Grandpa in his coffin. No *way* was I going up to him, I was too afraid. I had never seen a dead body. As soon as I kissed Wanda, I got as far away from his coffin as I could and stayed in my seat until the service started.

Soon, however, it was my turn to go up to the microphone, which was next to the casket. I had never been so scared. I made my way up the carpeted aisle and kept my eyes down. The walk seemed to take forever. When I finally got up there and turned to face the sorrowing crowd, I snuck a sideways peek at Dale's body, just a few feet away. The peek lingered into a stare, and the stare slipped into a long moment as I just stood there, gaping at my grandpa's pale, lifeless face. It felt like an eternity, but it probably lasted about five seconds.

Finally, instead of beginning my speech, I whispered

into the mic, "I've never seen a dead body before." Another long moment. "And now, seeing him, I realize he's not here. That body is only a shell, and that shell has nothing to do with us when we leave it." This staring, whispering girl, grappling with existence itself, was not the polished representation of the family my mom had probably hoped for, but I couldn't help it.

I finally turned my eyes back to the mourners and began my speech the way I was supposed to. "I'd like to honor my grandpa by reading one of his letters; he wrote it to my grandma while he was in the war. His words, which I will read exactly as written, are a beautiful reflection of the person he was, and what better way to be remembered than by our own words?"

Paris area, France
Sat Eve. 6:30 PM
3 feb. 1945

Hello my Darling—
I'm writing this from the office, I'm in charge of Quarters tonite, The fellow that had C.Q. wanted off so I told him I would take it. I'll get caught up on some of my letter writing maybe, getting my mail all at one time makes it a little hard to answer everybody right away + of course I'll write you if I don't anybody else. You come first always, you know that. Well I've been off to-day, But didn't do anything especially. Tell Guyneth I got her a nice bottle of perfume this afternoon + Will send out another box in the near future, just as soon as I get some more things gathered up, I know what I'll

get for Susie + you but have to figure out something for Burb. But will have it on its way in a couple of days. I only hope you have received my Xmas box by now, it has been sent almost 2 months now, The way they handle boxes though it might have got all broken up, although I did have it packed + tied up good. I hope it has warmed up some back there honey, the weather here has cleared up + warmed up til we hardly needed any fire to-day. But will probably break loose again before long. How is everybody at home sweetie? Here I go again blowing off plus I never asked you how you were? I hope you were OK. I'm just fine + was very happy to receive four nice letters from you, written on the 8th of Jan, I think you must of had your dates mixed up a little, you were writing on Sun nite + Sun was the 7th. But that's OK just so long as you write, another on the 9th in fact two on the 9th, You are just my doll for thinking about me + writing so good + the last one on the 10th of Jan. The one you wrote on sun, You had been down home all day, I'm sure glad you could go down + I know the folks were plenty glad to see you. Wish I could've been there with you. The hunting sounds good, but most of all I would want just you, the heck with the hunting. Funny about the pictures, I was going to have some taken to-day, But the studio it was closed, so will have them taken the first of the week, it takes about two weeks to get them back here. But will send you one as soon as I can, I'm glad Macy got some from DB. In your letter of Tues morning you said you had been to the Orpheum to a show the night before, (by yourself) no guilty concentious? If they would give me a rowboat I'd start back to you tonight. I'm glad you do get out sweetie you must get pretty lonesome + disgusted sometimes, I'll try + do my part + keep the letters coming to you + maybe that will help some. How about those teeth? Honey do you have enough money? I don't get much, but if you need it I can sure get along on less, in fact none if I thought it would help you any. Don't never hesitate writing to me about things like that, after all you know I am your husband, and I'll prove it to you when I get back. Sure too bad about the Kerott boys, But that's the sacrifice some of us have to pay. I only hope it won't happen in vain. That is a good picture of the Peabody boys. Hope I get to see some of the fellows before long. Did you help your mom move? Hope she has something she likes better now. I doubt if she will ever feel at home anyplace only out there on the farm though. That was hers + your dad's whole life out there. Watch her pretty close my dear + don't let her get down sick. So Howard's girl thinks you look like her girlfriend, well sweetie i've been in Scotland, England, Ireland + France + I've never seen anybody that looked as lovely as you do in those pictures you sent in your letter, I have them right here in front of me now, I love you so much. I wouldn't blame anybody for looking at you, but if I ever catch them I'd knock their heads in. Jealousy, yes I guess so, but that's the way I am + you can't change me now. Or don't you want me to change anyway? You may want to trade me off for a new model when I get back. Don't mind me sweetie, I'm only blowing off. I hope. You sent that little clipping about the show in Paris, a lot of the fellows saw it, + I

REMEMBER ME AS HUMAN

guess it was real good. But I didn't go in, I think maybe I'll go to Paris to-morrow nite + see a show, I'll write + tell you all about it. Wish you were here to go with me, I'd enjoy it a lot more. To get back to the pictures you sent, they were really swell, it made me really homesick to see the house + surroundings, and little Susie is a regular doll, she is sure growing up, + you look about 19 you sweetie pie. Tell Guynie she looks plenty good to me. She will have to carry a club along with her, when she gets some of this Chanel perfume on that I got for her. Not that she smells bad now, but U know. Ha ha. Will close now honey, hope I see you in my dreams tonite. Take real good care of yourself for me + I'll do the same for you. Kiss Susie for me + tell Burb + Guynie hello. Good-nite lovely, with all my love + kisses. Your husband

The letter was perfect, it made people laugh and cry, especially Wanda. I was so glad; I wanted so much to help her somehow. As I passed the coffin, I glanced a final goodbye at the face I knew and loved so well. *Well done, Grandpa, we did it!*

———

AFTER WANDA AND I left the cemetery, I took her to our family's longstanding staple of existence, Dairy Queen. Her *favorite*. Even though we hadn't eaten lunch yet, we agreed ice cream was what we needed. Wanda ordered the same thing every time, a chocolate-dipped Dilly Bar. We ate and laughed and sang as we drove the deserted highway back to the nursing home. She was perfectly carefree. I'll always remember it.

After lunch in the dining room with the silent gang, we were back in her room with the camera rolling again.

Lucy: Okay, Grandma, I have some fun, lighter questions to ask you. What's your favorite color?

Wanda: My favorite color is orchid, or lavender.

Lucy: What's your favorite food?

Wanda: I like most everythin', I wasn't a big eater, never was…but my favorite I have to say is I like biscuits an' gravy.

Lucy: What is your favorite prayer, if you pray?

Wanda: Oh, my gosh, yes, ten million times I've prayed. "Our father which art in heaven, hallowed be thy name. Thy kingdom come, thy will be done on earth as it is in heaven. Give us this day our daily food and forgive us our trespassers. As they who trespass against us, and lead us not into temptation but deliver us from all evil', an'…accountable things."

Lucy: What's your favorite way to talk to God?

Wanda: Well, I just say, "Dear God, please help me. Please help me all you can at a time like this."

Lucy: Did you always pray like that?

Wanda: Well, I always felt that way, but especially now, because Dale has been taken from me. An' I also used to pray a lot because little Kathy was slow. I had to stay close to God in order to receive what I asked him for, an' he was as good to me as he could be.

Lucy: What were some important rules in your parents' house?

Wanda: My mom was very, very good at…"Don't

show your nakedness." She always said that. We was never allowed to even take a bath around each other in the old washtub. We all bathed on a Saturday, but we took turns, because there was only room for one of us at a time. We had to use the water sometimes three an' four times. Mom was always overseein' the whole thing, to see that we held our decency. She called it "decency," because that's what it was. She always upheld that, she was brought up that way herself, so therefore she turned out her children that way, too.

Lucy: What do you think is the most important thing in marriage?

Wanda: Bein' true to your loved one, that is the main thing, bein' very true to your loved one. There's so much philanderin' an' "wickedness" that goes on, as my mom would call it, an' "wickedness" is what it is. So in my marriage, I just remained decent about my joke tellin' an' my body. I didn't go around flashin' myself to men or boys or nothin', because I wasn't brought up that way. I was brought up in a motherly, good way...I learned the "why-fors" from the "bad-fors."

With these questions, I was slowly building up to ask about something that had been in my mind since I'd visited her family's farm two days earlier.

CHAPTER FOURTEEN

Lucy: Can you tell me about how your father died?

Wanda: Well, he took his own life, hon. My dad hung hisself in the barn. But the coroner said that he had actually had a heart attack, as soon as he found out that he was on the stepladder to choke him to death. My mom and I had been watchin' him real close those days, because he had gotten into some insecticide we put on the leaves of our cabbage to keep the bugs off, an' it's deathly poison. Dad had went to the cob shed [an outbuilding made of sand, clay, and straw] an' got into the bug poison. Mom knew that Dad was failin' up here, up in the upper story [points to her head]. When he took the poison, her an' I fed Dad full of milk for his stomach an' brought him back to life from the bug poison that he sneaked out of the cob shed an' took.

So then the mornin' he did take his life, he got up out of their bed downstairs, an' 'course all of us kids slept upstairs…an' he sneaked out of the bed an' went to the barn, put up the rope, got everythin' ready, an' then that's when the coroner said he did not die of suffocation of the throat…he died of seein' what he had got hisself into.

This seems like a kindness on the coroner's part, to lessen the devastation for the family, but I could see Wanda believed it completely.

Lucy: And wasn't Grandpa Dale with you that night?
Wanda: Yes, he was. He was upstairs in an open bed, an' I was in the parlor room downstairs next to my folks. He stayed all night because when he brought me home from wherever we went on a date, I said, "You don't need to drive into town, it's too late. Go upstairs an' crawl in bed with one of my brothers, he's just takin' up a whole bed, you might as well accompany him." So that's what he did. So that mornin' Dad took his life, yes, Dale was there, Dale was there.

But I don't tell everybody about Dad takin' his life, I don't tell everybody. Because…well, for certain reasons you don't go back over somethin' that you didn't want to ever think about again, much less talk about. But of course, every once in a while it comes for us. An' of course, if people are still livin' that lived around that time, why, they would remember it, too, you know. You can't keep away from gossip an' news, you can't keep away from it. An' the gossip is mean.

Yes, my Great-Grandfather Frank Roughton committed suicide. It happened on April 16, 1940, not long after my grandparents started dating. Dale and Wanda had gone out dancing a few towns over, and arrived back at her family's farm, where she'd been living since her divorce from Henry, about one a.m. Just before sunrise, my Great-Grandma Nellie woke the whole house in a panic. Wanda recalls she was screaming, "Frank's not in his bed, I'm afraid he's done it this time!"

Everyone leaped out of their beds, and in the freezing-cold darkness, they searched the creaking house and the frosty grounds for Frank. There were so many places to look, several barns, a dozen outbuildings, and the wooded areas that dotted the property.

What happened next was truly gruesome for everyone present, but especially for my grandfather, since he is the one who found Frank. When Dale threw open the heavy wooden doors to one of the barns and shone his light inside, Frank was there hanging from a rafter. My quiet, sweet grandfather found his would-be father-in-law's lifeless body dangling from a rope around his neck.

The horror Dale must have felt in that moment, and then having to alert the others, would've been an indescribable shock. Imagine, you're just beginning to date someone, and you are the one to discover their parent dead from suicide. It might make you want to take care of that person forever. I suspect Dale felt that way, for he married Wanda just two months later, on June 25.

I couldn't tell you how I ended up with it, but I have in my possession my Great-Grandfather Frank's suicide note from that very night. It's written on a simple postcard, the kind you buy at a souvenir shop to send home from your vacation. On one side, it has pictures of Native American adobe villages and a popular cowboy poem called "Out Where the West Begins," written in 1917 by Arthur Chapman.

Out where the hand-clasp's a little stronger,
Out where the smile dwells a little longer,
That's where the West begins.
Out where the sun shines a little brighter,

REMEMBER ME AS HUMAN

Where the snows that fall are a trifle whiter,
Where the bonds of home are a wee bit tighter,
That's where the West begins.

Out where the skies are a trifle bluer,
Where friendship ties are a little truer,
That's where the West begins.
Out where a fresher breeze is blowing,
Where there's laughter in every streamlet flowing,
Where there's more of reaping and less of sowing,
That's where the West begins.

Out where the world is still in the making,
Where fewer hearts with despair are breaking,
That's where the West begins.
Where there's more of singing and less of sighing,
Where there's more of giving and less of buying
And a man makes friends without half trying,
That's where the West begins.

And on the back side, where you're supposed to write to your loved ones that you're having a wonderful time and you'll see them soon, Frank penciled his final goodbye.

Dear Nellie best little wife i am no good enny more get some one that has some Brains sell the place. before old carson gets it away from you. and take the money go to Florda. with Guyneth and live as happy as you can but bee sure and come back and lay with me by little Harold don't forget he lives above good bye and god bless you. pray for me i have stood all i can for the last three months F. Hudson FR $1440

Nothing in that note is a typo; it is exactly as Frank spelled and punctuated it. I often hold the postcard in my hands and ponder his reasoning: $1,440—the amount baffles me. After that sum, he wrote two words that I cannot for the life of me decipher. *Dont rent? Doubt rent?* Are they the answer? I don't know. Did he take his life over $1,440? In 1940, $1,440 would be equivalent to some $26,053 today. Although the Roughton family had some money to speak of, Frank apparently was constantly in debt. Roughton legend is that he gambled the farm away in a card game, to a man named Carson.

When I was young, I was categorically judgmental about suicide. I was very scared by the story of my Great-Grandfather Frank's hanging, and, on the Walsh side of my family, equally scared by my Grandmother Helen's suicide when I was fourteen. Suicides on both sides of my family has made for some late-night contemplation, that's for sure. My young, naive mind used to protect itself from this fear by labeling anyone who committed suicide an insane monster, and I wrote them off as incredibly selfish.

Then, as I turned thirty, one of my close friends, Johnny Lewis, killed himself. When he did that, I was forced to rethink my opinions on the matter, because I knew this person's heart, and he was no monster. Nor was he some much older person I couldn't relate to. He was my age. We had shared many a Dark Night of the Soul; in fact, he had helped me through one tough emotional time in particular, pulling me through the pain of a devastating breakup when I needed it most. I'll always remember him ordering me off the couch where he'd let me blubber on his shoulder for days, making me go on a walk with him to point out things in the neighborhood that had nothing to do with my pain. His selfless support is what got me moving forward again. How could he have become helplessly lost in that darkness himself? *I could've walked with you, Johnny. Why didn't you come to me, beautiful friend?*

I knew he must've fought against his demons as much as he could, and it was impossible to condemn or dismiss him for losing the battle. It made me very confused by my old tired beliefs on the subject, and my longstanding condemnation began to unravel. His suicide allowed me to shift my perspective on my own family's suicides, no longer needing to fear or resent them. I really thank you, Johnny, for that transformative life lesson.

As I've emotionally matured deeper into empathy and away from fear-based judgment, I've come to feel that suicide could be described as "death by depression." Depression is very real, something everyone feels at one time or another. I don't pretend to have a clinical understanding of suicide, nor a grasp on the infinite scenarios and reasons why people take their own lives, but I do know that I no longer judge those who die from it. We all have our demons, and demons are always sniffing at the door, listening, waiting.... All we can do is stick together. I hold all those who have died by suicide in my heart and with mercy.

Those who are left behind make the common mistake of torturing ourselves over what we could've done, should've done to save them. But we humans are masters at hiding our depression when we want to, and can appear to be the happiest person in the room. It's a sick game to punish yourself for not seeing when someone is doing that. I think what we can do, what is in our power to do, is to stand for shining a light on problems that people and society as a whole try to gloss over; to strive to create safe spaces for one another where we can share our feelings and challenges.

The other dangerous part of the emotional aftermath is struggling to figure out *why*. I have to stop myself from doing that now with my great-grandfather. How could Frank leave his wife alone with their eleven children? Why did he feel so hopeless over money? Why couldn't he have just had a good meal and a good nap to put things into perspective? My fixes for him seem so simple. Get a loan! Go to rehab! Stop gambling! Get a good night's sleep! Naive of me, I know. We're so arrogant with our solutions for other people, aren't we? The truth is, suicide leaves us with questions that can never be answered.

Suicidal or not, most of us have had moments in our lives when we've thought, "Anything is better than this." Clearly, my Great-Grandfather Frank Roughton yearned to be in a happier place. The poem on his suicide note conveys a notion of sanctuary and hope, a better tomorrow.

With his final words, Frank advised his wife on what to do after his death, still striving to make things okay for her. Nellie did not do as Frank instructed, however; she did not go to Florida. Maybe she wasn't brave enough, maybe she was too heartbroken over her husband's death to leave the world they had built together. She remained on the farm and carried on, then moved to town and I'm sure did her best to live a happy life until she died fourteen years later, in 1954. One thing is as Frank requested: Nellie does lie next to him and their little Harold. I write this now, sitting at their graves, and run my finger over their simple inscriptions on cold marble: "Mother," "Father," "Son."

Another whirlwind of human drama come to a close, buried and forgotten under the unassuming fields.

Lucy: Were you angry at your dad for doing that?

Wanda: No, no, no, an' neither was Mom. She did think Dad should've stayed here a lot longer, because of such a family we had to care for, an' she couldn't hack everythin'…she had good reason to feel that way. But, uh, she took care of it real well after he passed away, so everythin' went along as good as could be expected. An' Mom had still never gotten over my little brother Harold dyin' from the school accident, so she just sat an' cried, an' cried, an' cried. It didn't do any good, because Dad was gone an' Harold was gone.

Lucy: Look at all the people she had around her; she had all you other kids. She still had a lot to be happy for, I hope.

Wanda: Yes, she did, she had plenty to do all the time, plenty to do.

Lucy: What would you say to people my age about life?

Wanda: Well, the thing is, people your age are workin' every day to find somethin' to do…to put their life into gear an' make it worthwhile. That strivin' is good, but we also got to accept what the good Lord feels fit to give us, an' be happy with what we can be happy with. Because…that happiness means that you went out of this world with lots of friends an' lots of relations that you really cared for…really, really cared for.

Life will constantly refer you back to your ancestors… just as my ways center on my mom, an' you kids' ways center on your mom an' me. All your habits, all your ways, all your talk, all your personality, it will all center on your ancestors as time goes.

Lucy: What do you think happens when we pass over?

Wanda: Well, I'll just leave this world, hon, onto the next place.

Lucy: Do you think your mom will be waiting for you, and your husband, and all your brothers and sisters?

Wanda: I hope so, I hope so. I'd like to see 'em all.

Lucy: Were you with your mom when she passed?

Wanda: Sure, I was right there. She had gone blind, but she had neighbors an' family all around her that loved her. Each one of us daughters was takin' care of her wants an' needs, right there on Glover Street where she lived. She was so sick an' dyin', but we loved bein' able to care for her. She closed her eyes, breathed her last breath, an' was gone. An' there was Guynie, Ethel, me, an' Violet…all of us girls were there. Also some nieces. It was quite a houseful of those who loved her the same as I did.

Lucy: What was the last conversation you had with her?

Wanda: Well, on her death bed, she said, "Wanda Mae, you have no business bein' down here takin' care of an old woman, when you have your little girls to think about." That was Kathy an' your mom Jody, they was just so high [holds her hand a foot above the ground] when Mom died. I said, "Mom, we will not go into that. You have done for all of us, an' you are not to talk that way, it is just against the rules of your life."

She said, "Well, I'm sorry, honey, but I've got to talk to someone about this an' that, some tough things, an' I can't burden you." I said, "You go right ahead an' you say what you want to say, because I'm here to take care of your last wishes. I'm stayin' right here with you until the end." We told each other how much we loved each other.

Lucy: That sounds very peaceful.

Wanda: Very peaceful it was. She was always so understandin', the things she understood in others was amazin', amazin'. My mom was always happy to make friends with 'most everyone, an' so am I. She was such a thoughtful woman. I hope I gave the same to her in the end.

Lucy: It's been a long time since she left you, hasn't it?

Wanda: A looooong, long time. An' all my sisters an' brothers are gone, too, I'm the only one left. I don't know why the good Lord has left me here so long.

Lucy: What would you like people to know about you?

Wanda: I'm just the way the good Lord an' my mom an' dad made me. I'll never change. An' to know that I always had silly expressions to make people laugh, that I couldn't help myself, that's just the way I lived.

Lucy: How would you like your life to be remembered?

Wanda: That I made it as good as I possibly could make it.

Lucy: Well, Grandma, our interview is over. Is there anything else you'd like to say?

Wanda: Take it a day at a time, honey, an' a night at a time, that's the only way you can take it.

––––––

MY GRANDMOTHER'S WORDS HUNG in the air as she sat in her wheelchair, staring into space. I watched her and waited to see if she was going to continue, as she so often did after very long silences, but she wasn't saying anything more, and I realized her advice was final. Sounds outside the room brought me back to the present day. The same cross-chiming of alarms, pitched voices of nurses, scattered coughing of neighbors in the surrounding rooms flooded in again as our talk came to an end.

"Thank you for letting me interview you, thank you," I said as I rose and began to turn off the recording equipment. Wanda was also slow coming back to reality, and as she wheeled herself to the bathroom, she said over her shoulder, "Put the room back together, hon."

I took my time. My work was done, but I didn't want to leave her. My entire life, Wanda had treated every single goodbye as if it were the last. Our farewells on her front porch when I was a child went on for an hour as she blubbered and kissed each kid and my parents fifty times. At the time, I mocked her, but young people don't understand goodbyes. She never took our visits for granted and savored every moment.

Now, we slowly headed down the hallway toward the front door, and for the first time, she had nothing to say. When we finally reached the front desk, she asked me to help her from her wheelchair onto the brown bench where I had found her waiting for me each day. I helped her get situated, and then I knelt down on my knees for our final goodbye. She pressed her forehead to mine, our noses touching, and took my face in her hands.

"I love you, sweetie," she said tearfully, in a true whisper for the first time.

"I love you" was all I could manage.

We stayed like that, holding each other's faces, for a long moment. I finally stood up and thanked the nurses, and though I felt weak and did not want to leave her, I found my resolve and walked through the exit doors.

As they swung closed behind me, I looked back through the glass one last time and watched her sitting there, so small, her hands folded in her lap, murmuring to herself. What was she saying? I squinted, straining my eyes to read her lips, and I realized that she wasn't talking; she was singing. I kept reading her lips, studying the rhythm she swayed to, until I recognized the song. It was "Tiptoe Through the Tulips." Of course it was. Harold's song.

I watched her sing a song that connected her to a place and a time when she was in the midst of life, when loneliness was just an occasional visitor. Now loneliness was a constant companion, beckoning her to succumb. She never did, though. She fought it tooth and nail, in every way, every day and every night; from her gorgeous outfits, her perfectly done-up hair and makeup, her crooked-fingered piano playing, her beloved stuffed animals, her portable radio through the long nights, her proper dining-room etiquette, her care for her neighbors in that home whether they appreciated it or not, her surprise snack box, her JOKES—all those things were Wanda's staring loneliness in the face, spitting on its outstretched hand, and telling it to fuck off for today.

My Grandmother Wanda stood for making the most out of the time we are given. She stood for fighting against the darkness with positivity and humor. She stood for never giving up. And this she taught me by example, for even as I left her sitting on her bench to face the loneliness, she sang.

CHAPTER FIFTEEN

THOSE THREE DAYS I spent with Wanda was indeed our last goodbye. When death started to grip her, only four months later, she kept telling my mom Jody that the only reason she was still hanging on was because she worried about the pain and grief my mom would feel.

"Oh, Mom, you can go," Jody assured her repeatedly. "I don't want to lose you, but I don't want you to be worried about that at all." How beautiful that in my family are generations of women reassuring one another on their deathbeds that it's okay to let go. May we all be so supported in love in our last moments.

I like to think our interview had something to do with Wanda's feeling ready to leave us. She never said anything more about it, but maybe it gave her some peace, knowing that her story was safe now.

With my mom's help, Wanda planned every detail of her funeral. They talked about how she wanted her hair done (you guessed it, a lacquered bubble), the music, even that she'd like her top lip plumped up with an injection. She did not want a certain mortuary cosmetologist to be the one to prepare her for her viewing, though, because she hadn't liked the woman. That made me laugh, as I imagined what had gone down between the two to cause such animosity. There will always be stories that we never get the chance to hear. I know that now.

Wanda wanted to be buried in a rose-pink pantsuit.

Looking everywhere for the perfect outfit, my mom walked into a Ross, of all places, and there it was, hanging on an otherwise empty rack. She took it back to Wanda, who studied it an inch from her face, then exclaimed with her four-tooth grin, "Oh, it is perfect!"

After that, Wanda really started to go. As her organs began to fail, and there was nothing to be done except keep her comfortable, she was moved from the nursing home to the Carle Foundation Hospital in Urbana. Mom called me on her way to the airport to say she was flying back to Illinois to try to make it to Wanda's side.

The thought of her mother dying before she got there was unbearable, and she was panicked. "I just keep praying over and over that she'll wait for me."

I replied gently, "Mom, I believe that people decide who will be with them when they pass. Sometimes they choose to be alone, and sometimes they choose to have certain people there…. However she wants it to be, it's already taken care of."

This calmed her, and she got to Wanda about midnight on Monday, May 16, 2011.

It was then that my mom called me, and I heard my grandmother one last time. She wasn't opening her eyes anymore, and she had stopped speaking, but she was moaning and groaning like an animal. Mom put the phone to Wanda's ear, and I told her I loved her entirely, and my heart was right there with her; I told her that she was safe. I hope she heard me. All I heard was her panting, very sharp, labored breaths where she could take them between groans.

When Mom hung up, I was physically alone in the

darkness of my bedroom, but every other part of me was with Wanda, holding her in my soul as she was pushed from this realm to the next by that unseen force that we humans have zero capacity to understand.

I stayed on my bed for a long time, my senses heightened, my total being focused on my grandmother. I had a candle lit, time passed, I didn't move until I jumped from my trance several hours later when my mom called to say that Wanda was gone. "I am still sitting here with her body; it just happened."

I heard a long-held breath escape my lips with a guttural croak.

Mom continued, slowly and blissfully, as if recalling a beautiful dream. "It was just my mom and me in the hospital room. She was lying still with her eyes closed, the panting had stopped, and I sat next to the bed and kept my hands on her legs, saying, 'Mom, you can go any time. I'm here, you can go.' With my hands still on her legs, I put my head down on her bed and faded in and out of sleep. Then I realized she wasn't going to leave as long as I was physically holding onto her. I knew she wouldn't let go until I did. I was so afraid, but I knew I had to let her be, so I moved to a chair across the room, where I could see her silhouette in the darkness. I would close my eyes for a few moments, and then open them with a start to see her chest still rising and falling. It wasn't long until I looked up and realized that her chest wasn't rising anymore."

Jody alerted the nurses and doctors to record the time of death, three-twenty-five a.m., and then she called me. Through tears, I told her, "See, Mom, you made it! She meant for it to be just you two." What an honor it is to be with someone as they take their last breath.

I marveled at how very similar the processes of birth and death are: the physical and mental exertion, the miraculous transformation, the releasing and embracing, all at once. Acceptance. Mother witnesses child's first breath; child witnesses mother's last. Exactly as it should be. From my bed thousands of miles away, with candlelight flickering on the murky walls until the lengthening blue dawn arrived, I wept at the enormity of it all.

————

TWO DAYS LATER, I flew back to Illinois for Wanda's viewing at the Renner Wikoff Chapel, in Urbana. Established in 1875, it was a single-story red-brick and white-pillared building, like a mini-plantation. My grief made me want to burn it down. I was very nervous about seeing Wanda's body, just as I had been for Dale. I was in no rush to get face to face with it, and I moved at half-speed to the room where the open white coffin was.

As I entered, I hated everything I saw. Grief makes everything hateful. The space was carpeted in blue-gray drab, had low ceilings, and felt very claustrophobic. Two chandeliers cast a soft florescent glow over the room like in a department store. I wondered why they had to light it that way. Tacky. Grief makes everything tacky. While there were some tasteful, classical-looking paintings on the walls, it all felt sterile and bland, like the nursing home had been. Grief makes everything bland.

Although my sorrow made me angry at the whole

room, it was beautifully lined with flower wreaths and blown-up photos of Wanda on wooden easels. Under Wanda's direction, Mom had done a gorgeous job of decorating it. It was a stunning tribute.

Wanda's casket was at the far end of the room. I tentatively made my way toward the coffin, trying to appear casual and unaffected, but I couldn't breathe; my chest was heavy with panic, and my heart was pounding. As I got closer, I could see my grandma's porcelain-white face peeking over the rim of the casket. Then I was there. I peered down at her. A wave of shock froze me, as if my brain had put up a wall of numbness to shield me from the sight. It took a few seconds to register what I was seeing.

Hello again, Grandma. She was perfectly put together, just like always. Signature red lipstick (gorgeous, plump upper lip, as requested), red nail polish, perfectly bubble-fluffed white hair, rose-pink pantsuit, jewelry, the whole shebang. In the coffin with her was her favorite orange-cat stuffed animal and, of course, a paperback book of jokes.

I stood there looking at her body for a long time. The face I knew so well and loved so much. People came and went past the coffin, but I wasn't paying attention. My mom's arm was around me at one point, and I tried to comfort her back, but it was hard to do anything other than stand there, perfectly still, lost in Wanda's face and folded hands. Her pale skin looked so incredibly delicate, as if any touch stronger than a feather would rip it. So when I reached out and touched her face, I tried to be as soft as that. The delicacy had been an illusion, for her skin was cold and hard, like plastic. I smoothed her hair, I held her folded hands, I noticed how the dark blue veins showed under the skin, full of a preservative now. All was cold, all was perfect.

As my shock wore off, I began to hate the room a little less. Her dead body was actually fascinating, but I felt like a creep for even thinking it. I wondered if I was the only person in the room who was curious about death in this way. It was like I wanted to understand death as much as I possibly could while it was physically in front of me. Grief makes you think bizarre things.

I even looked further into her coffin. To my amazement, I saw that her feet were bare. Obviously, she didn't need shoes, and I'm sure the funeral directors didn't expect anyone looking down there, but I immediately wished I hadn't, because I saw something that upset me more than anything else that day. Her feet were black. The sight almost did me in, and I yanked my head back up. She looked fine up top, as if sleeping, but her feet exposed the truth that this was not my grandma anymore, just the shell her soul had left behind.

My curiosity about her body that day was my way of coming to terms with her death, of course, and with death in general. I was proud of the progress I had made since Dale's funeral. We each have our own way of dealing with death, and mine that day was to make friends with it, try to feel less afraid of it. At the casket, my mom, my sister, and I shared a moment I'll always remember, and then I leaned down and put my forehead to Wanda's for one long, last time. *Until we meet again, Grandma.*

After Wanda's death, I inherited the electric keyboard she had played in her room for me. Cousin Talor generously shipped it to me in California, and I'm so grateful she made sure I was the one in the family to have it. I arrived home one day to find the large, heavy box on my doorstep. As I hauled it inside, the keyboard somehow turned itself on inside the box and began playing one of its programmed demo songs at top volume.

"Okay, Grandma, I'm hurrying, hang on!" I yelled as I ran to get a knife. In life, Wanda couldn't WAIT for the music to start. I'm so glad death hasn't changed that.

AFTERWORD

2020, IN THE MIDST of writing the book.

A dream.

Wanda and I stood face to face in a darkened room. Other beings encircled us, but I couldn't make out who they were. We stood in the center of the circle, and she held my hands in hers. She was strong, ageless, a serene smile on her face and joy in her eyes. "I want to tell you how to finish your book," she said.

"Great!" I blurted out. "I am a bit stuck."

She looked amused. "I know you been wonderin' how to do it, hon."

"Yes!" I exclaimed. "I've been struggling with how much detail to share about the family, about you, and I don't think I know how to do it."

She looked deep into me. "You must tell the truth. That's your answer."

Silence.

"All of it?" I asked.

"Yes," came her insistence.

Another silence.

"Even the one thing?"

She leaned in. "Especially the one thing."

Careful to word my concerns correctly, I ventured, "But it makes you look bad."

"NO," she replied as her lips curled into a big smile. "It makes me look *human*. And I want to be remembered as human."

APPENDIX

My Grandfather Dale was twenty-nine when he was drafted into World War II. He and my Grandmother Wanda had been married less than three years. Leaving behind not only Wanda but his first child, Susie, born not long before he shipped out, and Burb, a lively eight-year-old boy from Wanda's first marriage, he served from 1943 until the very end of the war, in late 1945. His service took him from Ireland and England to just behind the front lines in France. During the three years they were separated, he and Wanda wrote each other hundreds of letters, sometimes more than one or two a day.

While every last one of Wanda's letters failed to survive the war, having to be burned, sixty-three of Dale's letters home did survive and were given to me when I was seventeen. I have carefully chosen excerpts from forty-one of them, excerpts I feel are a particularly fascinating and intimate peek into both Dale's wartime experiences and his feelings for his wife and family. These are words he wrote only for her, never dreaming that one day, more than eighty years later, you would read them, too.

I know many families have their own treasured letters, written in wartime or peacetime, that offer a glimpse of their loved ones and the times they lived in, their own compelling documents of human history. I would love to hear from anyone who would like to share theirs. Write to me at RememberMeAsHuman@gmail.com.

Excerpts from Dale's letters:

Monday eve. 10:30 PM
3 July 1944

   Just returned to the barracks after playing nine innings of baseball and am pretty well tired out. I don't think I'll even shave too night, if they don't like it they know what they can do. You won't want me to shave every day when I get back will you?

Somewhere in N. Ireland
Wed night, 9:00 pm
5 July 1944

   Im thinking alot about our trip to Texas, the evening I walked upstairs in that house and there you were standing in your stocking feet, looking like a million dollars and waiting for me to give you a big kiss.
   Yes we've been married four years my darling, and

REMEMBER ME AS HUMAN

how fast those years have gone. It seems like only yesterday I first saw you and to think that we have a beautiful little daughter almost two years old. God, how glad I'll be when this thing is over and I can get back to you again and forever.

Im writing this letter from the office as I'm charge of quarters again tonight. I have your letters laying in front of me on the desk and will read them again before I go to bed. I hope you had a good 4th and I wish I could've been there with you. I celebrated by working all day and sold tickets for drinks at a party the officers had last night. I drank one beer and one shot, im saving all my celebrating until I get home and can have you with me.

Someplace in N. Ireland
Thurs nite 10:30 pm
6 July 1944

We played ball this evening, It was raining part of the time, but we played just the same. And the officers beat us, but it was very enjoyable. We had a little bet on this evening, the officers invited the enlisted men up to their mess hall for sandwiches and coffee after the game and the losers had to wash the dishes afterwards, so we were stuck. It was about ten 'o clock when we got back to the barracks, and I tried to clean out my barracks bags a little. They are going to be plenty heavy as it is. There's one thing I really hate to do and that is to burn all your lovely letters my dear. I have two big boxes of them and I can't say how much each one of them has meant to me.

Tues nite 10:00pm
25 July 1944

We moved today and we now have a roof over
our heads. How long we'll stay here, noone knows,
because things are moving pretty fast now. I fixed a
little shelf on the foot of my bed and have my lovely
wife and daughters pictures on it, so I can look at you
the last thing at night and the first thing when I wake
up in the morning.

Sat night 8:30 PM
26 Aug 1944

I'm sure glad you received the pressed flowers in
my letter alright. The one you sent me in your letter
still had some smell left to it. It wasn't very much for
your birthday honey, but hope I can be with you the
next year and I'll give you a big kiss, besides other
things!! Bunkmate George is laying up here in his
bunk, eating some cookies out of a 'K' ration. They're
as hard as a rock, so I guess he must really be hungry.
A fellow can't expect too much now.

Sun nite 9:00 pm
27 Aug 1944

Went to church services today. A chaplain came
around in a jeep and we did services under a tree
here in camp. He held communion too, the first time
I've been to communion since I was a little boy. The
chaplain was very nice and it makes a fellow feel
pretty good just to sing and pray a little. Remember I
love you so much my Darling.

Thurs nite 8:00 pm
7 Sept 1944

There's a show here someplace tonite, but I didn't
go. I felt more like going out and finding a bottle.
Guess I must be sort of low. Last night I dreamed
I was home again and it was so real. I was really
disgusted when I woke up. Received my rations today,
we get 4 bars of candy now instead of 2 and 7 packs of
cigarettes. George trades me his candy for cigarettes.
I have plenty of cigarettes and I still smoke my pipe
quite a bit, the one you got me. But have been smoking
too much lately, so will have to cut down a little.

Sat. 3:00 pm
9 Sept 1944

Last night I saw a show "White Cliffs of Dover", see
it if you can darling, it was really good.

Tues nite 9:00 pm
12 Sept 1944

Was down to see Lt. Cumickey a while this evening.
Had a couple shots of scotch. I would really love you
to pieces if you were here now. Don't worry your
pretty head darling, I am being real good just for you.
I'll be back to you just as I left, because I love you too
much for it to be any other way. Its pretty chilly to-nite
so am going rite to bed. Hope I dream about you.

Friday nite 8:00pm
29 Sept 1944

Another month gone and it still looks as though

it might be quite a while before this thing is over. A fellow really gets fed up sometimes, but theres nothing to do only just sweat it out. And dream of the time to come when you can get home once more. I received my absentee ballot yesterday so I voted and sent it back. Be sure and vote if you can. I was looking at some of the pictures you had sent to me last nite and it made me feel bad to have to burn all your letters. I miss you more each day.

Sun nite 8:00 pm
8 Oct 1944

Today has been pretty rough. Our set up here is a little better than we have had in the past. At least we have cold running water in the billets and light part of the time. Don't worry your pretty head about anything. Ill write a long letter as soon as possible and tell you as much as I can. Ill have a time getting my clothes and everything straightened out now. They are in a mess Im sure. I haven't had on a tee or any blouse since we left Ireland. I hope I can find someone to do laundry for me. I had a nice dream about you last nite.

11 Oct 1944

I went to a French movie tonite with four other fellows. The short subjects were in English, but the main feature was entirely French, so we couldn't understand much. Finally we got up + come back to the barracks. It cost us eight francs or sixteen cents to get in. But it was well worth the price just to see the first part.

Friday nite
13 Oct 1944

Do you remember what we were doing about this time two years ago? I took you to the hospital about eight o'clock and little Susan was born at two on the fourteenth. And how proud I am of you both. Wish I could be with all of you tomorrow to help celebrate her birthday. I can just see the cake you'll have for her with the two little candles on it. I could use a carton or two of cigarettes sweetie, if you want to send me something. I'll try to send a box some of these days honey, when I get some things together for you.

15 Oct 1944

Im writing this from Red Cross. Its raining very hard today, which makes me very homesick for you. Wish you could see this Red Cross club, its really a very nice place. I'm sitting at a desk in the writing room, right next to the main entrance so I can keep an eye on the door. They have a radio playing in here. They serve coffee and donuts downstairs, but it is rather difficult to get a meal, as food is quite a problem in Paris right now. They also have an orchestra playing in one of the rooms, with flags and mirrors all over the place. I imagine it to be a big hotel from the looks of it. Im going to look in the register book after awhile and see if there's anybody's name is in it that I know.

How do you like this green paper? It was all I could get, so didn't think you would mind. You sure do write often sweetie and I really appreciate it a lot. As long as we are apart honey, letters are our only means of contact. And it is the only thing that will help to keep both our morales up. So as for my part I'll never let you down. I know our love is strong enough that we don't have to worry about anything else. If I didn't know you so well, I probably would be a little worried. But I'm not my darling. And someday everything will be ok again. I don't think I'll be too old when I get back, and I've been saving all my love just for you sweetie pie. I'll be back to you just as I left.

16 Oct 1944

I'm sending you some pictures sweetie. Some of the boys here have a dark room fixed up so they are doing some printing. Hope you like them. The fellow with me is Ed Corbett, he is a swell fellow. He has a little boy at home that he has never seen. This evening we had steak with onions. I thought of the swiss steak you used to make sweetie. We are eating off of plates right now instead of using mess glass. We also have a place close by where we can take a shower on weekends. So things are a lot better than they were for awhile. I guess we could put up with almost anything though, when you think of what the boys right on the front lines are having to contend with.

Sat Nite 8:30 pm
21 Oct 1944

I'm going to send a box so you will get it by xmas. Holidays don't mean much to me my darling, and I don't suppose they do to you either, but sometime we will celebrate not just the holidays but every day.

Im writing this in the day room, the radio is on and the music is very good, wish I could be dancing with you right now. I'll probably forget how by the time I get back. Some of the fellows are playing ping pong or shooting darts. There's not much else to do. I think its raining outside. Wish I could sit down and watch a good movie I think maybe they will get us some GI movies pretty soon. I got my laundry back this evening. The woman done a very nice job on it too, even patched my shorts where they were torn some.

And they don't want money, just some candy cigarettes or gum. So I gave her what I thought was right. Will be glad when this thing is over with and then I can start thinking about getting back to you honey. I'm afraid it's going to be quite a while, there's a lot of talk about demobilization and occupation troops, but guess I'll have to sit tight and listen. And when my turn comes to leave this damn country I'll be right there.

mon. nite 8:00 PM
23 Oct 1944

I have been reading, just finished "Camaron", it's very good. Worked all day yesterday, some of the fellows went to church, but the minister spoke entirely in French, so all they could do was just sit there + listen without understanding anything he was saying. It sure is chilly tonight. Wish you were here to keep me warm, You are just my doll. Guess I'll go down to the day room and listen to the radio a while and then go to bed. Hope to have a nice dream about you sweetie.

Wed
25 Oct 1944

I didn't write last nite because the special service officer arranged for us to go to a GI movie close by. They had two pictures, one a German propaganda picture & the other was "Paris honeymoon" with Bing Crosby. Its pretty old but I had never seen it so enjoyed it quite a lot. It was sort of a musical comedy. And Bing sang "You're a Sweet Little Headache" & another song or two, you know the ones they used to play on the music box at the Inn. It sure made me think of those days when I heard the songs again. This time last year I was in Pennsylvania. Remember I called you on the phone and talked to you? How glad I'll be when I can hear your sweet voice again, when I call you from New York or wherever I land.

Mon nite 8:00 PM
30 Oct 1944

I'm writing this in our day room here at the barracks. We have a fire in a little stove and the 'Ink Spots' are singing over the radio, so it is rather comfortable right now. Some of the fellows are sitting here playing cards and others reading or writing letters. It is real chilly out tonite, how I wish I were back in good old Urbana with you. It seems sometimes like this thing will never be over. But I guess I'm pretty lucky, so I shouldn't bitch. I see in the Stars and Stripes newspaper where Illinois almost beat Notre Dame. I sure would have liked to have been there and you and seen the game. A couple of the fellows and I went to a show last night. The short subjects were in English, but the main show was in French. James Cagney and Humphrey Bogart played, and there was enough action to it, until we could get the drift of it, even if we couldn't understand what they were saying. How I would enjoy to see a real good movie with you.

Thurs PM
2 Nov 1944

I sure enjoyed the clippings and pictures you put in your letters, you are so thoughtful. That's one of the many reasons why I married you. But of course the main one was because I loved you, don't ever forget that. And I will be so glad when the day comes that I can hold you in my arms once more.
What did you do Halloween honey? If someone had not mentioned the fact I would never even have thought about it. I sure remember the times we used to have on Halloween. But that sure seems so long ago now. Last night about twenty of the enlisted men got together in the day room and played twelve card games for about one hundred and fifty francs each. But unlucky me, I didn't win any. One fellow won four games I think. Oh well it was quite a bit of fun and helped to pass the time. It is really chilly in the barracks without any fire, a fellow has to go to bed to get warm. And what I hate worse than anything else is shaving in cold water. But I make the best of it. We got our rations today and only three packs of cigarettes a

week now. I need toothpaste very bad too. So if you send another box, send me some more toothpaste, a good toothbrush and honey when we moved positions here I lost one of the tees you sent me, remember? So if you can find any more of them, send me a couple and a collar clasp. You know, one of those with the springs on it. I lost that too. That's what this moving does to you. You really ruin to lose something every time. We had a bit of excitement here yesterday. Can't tell you anything now but will when I get home.

Mon nite 9:00 pm
6 Nov 1944

Well today is election day back there, when they get through with the political squabble in Washington, maybe the war will be over.

Wed nite 9:00 PM
8 Nov 1944

I'm down in the day room tonite. I can hardly write, with the radio on and all the noise. Most of the fellows are playing bingo. But I lost a hundred francs on the last game so I am not playing tonite. You said you had been to see the Sullivans. It was rather sad, but I thought it was true to life. I saw it while in Ireland. I'll bet you are having some swell fall days back there now. Those kinds of nights I dream about being back there with you. After supper is over I could help you with dishes. Then we would sit by the nice warm fire and listen to the radio or you could play the piano for me. You'll never know how much I miss all those things my dear. And sometimes it seems as though this thing will never be over. But maybe now the election is over and they quit horsing around back there in Washington, we can get down to the business of kicking the Germans around some more. That's going to be a pretty rough party in the Pacific too I think. I'm sort of worried, But hope everything will be OK.

Sat nite 9:00
11 Nov 1944

Well just twenty six years ago today the armistice was signed ending the first world war and now we are having to whip those bastards all over again. It sure is costing a lot of good lives to make up for the mistake we made once, so I hope it won't happen again. It sure is cold here. Some of the fellows had little stoves in their rooms, but they made them take them out because of the shortage of fuel. Its going to be a hard cold winter.

Mon nite 8:30
13 Nov 1944

Received a letter from you to-day, you had just gotten home from a Halloween party. I hope you had a good time there sweetie & would sure have liked to have been with you. I'll bet our daughter was cute all dressed up. She must be a regular doll. I know she will be changed a great deal when I get back, but I imagine we will all be somewhat different, that is only natural. All I ask though is just to get back to you honey & I know everything will adjust itself alright.

In a few more days I will be starting on my second year overseas. It seems like ages since I left you. I'm writing this in the day room, it's the only place around here with any heat in it. It used to be one big room, but they have changed it around and separated the writing room from the game room & it makes it a lot better. The boys are really getting some good out of it now. Most of the fellows are around here in the evenings, writing reading listening to the radio or playing ping pong. Honey, I hate to keep asking for things, but they have really cut our rations almost all off, I have plenty of soap & razor blades, but am short on toothpaste & cigarettes. We get one tube of toothpaste for eight weeks & this week we are getting no cigarettes at all. If it will help the combat boys some though, I can do without all the time. But I am afraid it's the black market racket in the states that is screwing things up. When I get home & someone spouts off about the soldiers getting everything, they'll get it right in the teeth.

Wed nite 9:00
15 Nov 1944

Goodnite, was going to say I wish you were here with me, but I don't. I imagine you would think about as much of this country over here as I do-and that's not much. Somehow sweetie I hope I am able to bring you back to Paris. Even now it's the most beautiful city I've ever seen and I know you would like it.

Thursday night 8:30
16 Nov 1944

Sure wish I could have been there to go to the
Urbana football game with you, I miss things like
that so much. But I want you to have a good time if
you can, you cant stay at home all the time and I trust
you always. You joked that I'm sweet for my Parisian
laundry woman?! 'Old Choppy' is about forty-five
and I gave her merchandise only. I have no desire to
cement the American, French relationships whatsoever.
So don't worry your pretty head my little doll.

Sun nite 9:00
19 Nov 1944

Well thanksgiving is almost here, and another one
away from my darling. When I stop to think that I've
started my second year overseas, it seems like ages
since I've seen you. But I'll keep my chin up as I know
you are doing and maybe it won't be too much longer.
These-damn lights just went out, so will try and finish
this by the light of my flashlight. Oh for the comforts
of home once more. I doubt if you'll be able to get me
out of the house sweetie when I do get back. And I'm
sure I won't need any raw eggs or oysters for quite
a while after I do get back. I'm saving it all for you
baby. Enough of that. I can use most anything honey,
cigarettes especially. Would like some lighter fluid
if you can find it in a tin can. Don't send it in glass.
I've almost got your box ready to mail, I can't get too
much as everything is so high, but hope you will like

it. You see, the way things are here now, the French franc is worth two cents in American money when it used to be worth twenty one cents. According to the prices of things, we should be getting about ten times as many francs as we do. I heard one of the officers telling today that he had eaten a meal in Paris. There was four or five of them and it cost them fifty-six dollars in American money* or twenty eight hundred francs in French money. So maybe that will give you some idea as to what we are up against. I'll thank God when I get back to the states where things are normal again. It sure bums me up when I read about those bastards stinking back there in those war plants. I'd sure like to have a few of them over here for a while. They would be glad to get back to the States and work for any price. Am going to wash a little (very little in this cold water) and go to bed. Guess I've blown off about enough.

*Nine hundred sixty-seven dollars in today's economy

Sat nite 7:30
25 Nov 1944

When I finish this letter I'm going to listen to the radio and then hit the hay. Most of the fellows are going to a dance, which lasts all nite. I'll just save my dancing, and when I get back we'll go out someplace and I'll step all over your feet. You better have some metal plates put on the toes of your shoes. I have been reading a very good book, "Leave Her to Heaven" by Ben Ames Williams. Have you been reading very much? I guess I'll try to go to church tomorrow afternoon, Id better go when I have the chance, because there is a lot of the time when we don't have a chaplain close by. Has your brother Paul shot any pheasants yet this fall? I sure would love to go hunting. Gosh I hope this thing winds up pretty shortly, but personally I think it will be spring now at least, and then I'll have to sweat out the demobilization setup after that. But some grand day my dear I'll be back to you.

Sun nite 8:00 pm
26 Nov 1944

Today I received your box full of goodies and it was really nice honey. I passed it around and everybody thought the cookies and candy was delicious. I still have the mints and fruit cake and will enjoy that sometime later. I cant thank you enough for all your trouble sweetie.

Wed nite 9:00 PM
29 Nov 1944

Last nite I played checkers with Billy Kohlmeyer and we each enjoyed a nice big piece of your cake before retiring. Everybody says it's the best fruitcake they ever tasted. Georgie and I ate some of it nite before last. So there's not too much left. The radio is on and they just announced that a mosquito plane just flew the Atlantic Ocean in 6 hours and 8 minutes. That sure is some speed. If I had one of those I would drop in for dinner with you on my day off. How about that? That would surely be the best thing I could ever ask for, would be to eat dinner with you on xmas day. I really get disgusted sometimes honey when I think of all the time I've been away from you and I really can't see the end in sight for quite a while yet. But remember my darling I'll always love you more than anyone else in the world. And I'll never do anything to hurt you. So just keep on loving me as I do you and I'll be back some day. And nothing will ever get me away from you again, until death do us part.

Christmas Eve 1944

This is the second Xmas I've had to be away from you my dear + I hope + pray it will be the last. I'm writing this from the offices, I have guard duty here tonight and is it ever cold. A merry Christmas to you all, God bless you.

Monday nite 8:00 pm
25 Dec 1944

Merry Christmas. I've been thinking about you all day honey. It was plenty cold & lonesome on guard last night. I just wondered where I would be that time next year. I remember when we used to have the program at the church at home the night before Christmas, one time we all went in the big wagon & it rained on us all the way there and back. All those things seem so far away now, just as though it might have been in another world. This is a poor Christmas for so many of the wives this year, but I know you all will make the best of it.

Sun. nite 9: pm
31 Dec 1944

I sure hope I won't still be writing to you this
time next year Sweetie. I hope I'm with you at home,
getting ready to do a little celebrating of our own.
There is quite a little cognac and champagne around
here this evening and I imagine things will get pretty
high by twelve o'clock. Will stay up until twelve
o'clock to see the end of the old year and the start of
the new one. This last year sure is one that I don't care
to remember.

I want to thank you so much for all you have done
for me during this last year, for all the swell letters,
the packages, taking care of everything back there at
home, for all your silent prayers and best of all your
love. That is enough to keep anybody on the straight
and narrow, I don't ever let myself think it can be any
other way. Happy New Year my dear.

Thurs nite 7:30 pm
4 Jan 1945

I don't see how these French people keep from all
dying of this cold. One of the fellows sent his laundry
out about ten days ago, so he went to see about it and
he said the one room this woman and her little girl
lived in was so cold he could hardly stand it. She was
trying to dry his clothes in there. They will probably
be dry about the fourth of july. I'll be so glad when I
can put something on but army clothes, I won't know
what to do.

Yesterday I got a Christmas card from my uncle with a new dollar bill in it. That good old American money sure looks good. I'll save it and when I get home we'll buy our first drink with it, ok?

Sat nite 9:00 PM
6 Jan 1945

How I wish I could've been with you tonite and every nite. I would hate to try to guess how much longer this thing is going to last, but I do know it's going to take a great deal more equipment and a lot of good lives. No matter how long my darling, please remember I'll be loving you every minute and I'm sure I can stick it out if you can.

I washed clothes this afternoon, don't know how they will be dry, I had them hanging outside, and when I went to bring them in this evening they were frozen stiff.

I sure would have liked to have seen you and your sister chasing that mouse. Which one was the mostest scared-you, her, or the mouse? Hate to think of you having to do things like fixing the doors and windows honey. When I get back I'll fix your breakfast for you and bring it to you in bed, how's that? Then we'll love some more.

The first thing after I get back, we are going house hunting and I don't mean maybe. Nothing but the best for the Boyers, right? Well we probably won't always have the best, but we'll have one another and as far as I'm concerned that's the best for me.

Tues nite 8:00 pm
9 Jan 1945

I hope you aren't getting too disgusted getting
along without me my dear, because our love and trust
means too much to both of us, being so far away from
one another for so long, for there ever to be any doubt.
Ive never been to Paris at night, because I visualize
what a drink or two can lead up to, so I just stay away
altogether. Every evening when I come home I always
sit on my bunk and look at your picture.

10:30 Sunday night
14 Jan 1945

Good morning my darling. If I were there at home
I would get up and fix the fires, get the funny papers
and then we would read them in bed together. I guess
I just like you sweetie. Sometimes I get so lonesome
and homesick to see you I can't hardly stand it, but
then I know its impossible until this damn war is over.
So I just have to think about you and what a grand
day it will be when I do get back to you. Is it ever cold
here now, think I'll put on all the clothes I can get on
me and pile the rest on my bed and then try to keep
warm. Keep your chin up darling.

Tues night 6:30 pm
16 Jan 1945

I'm writing this by candle light, no electricity here.
How is the rationing, can you get most anything you
need? please take care of yourself and get your teeth

worked on if they need it. I'll be lucky if I have any when I get back. This dehydrated food we have ruins them. And we don't get enough fresh fruits.

Sat pm 3:00
20 Jan 1945

Thought you might like this little clipping I cut out of the Stars and Stripes today...

"There was better news from Homer, Ill. Richard Duton, only barber in this village of 1,000 persons, got back from the Army. He'd been gone three months, and when the discharged soldier got off the train the entire long-haired town was there to cheer him. They paraded him to his barber shop where he donned a white coat, took barber tools from his suitcase and started to work."

I see by the papers that the army plans to take everybody that is not limited service and give them rifle practice and put them on the front lines and let some of the fellows up there get out of it for a while. If there's anything wrong with me I don't know what it is, so keep your fingers crossed and don't be surprised at anything.

Wed eve. 8:00 pm
31 Jan 1945

The radio is on here in the day room and the music is pretty good. Some of the fellows are playing cards and some are reading. Everybody crowds into two rooms in the evening because the rest of the rooms are so cold. You're frozen to death unless you are in bed. I still have to use my overcoat for a blanket at night. I think this is probably the hardest year the French people will ever be put through. The railroads and trucks are all hauling war materials, so everybody just freezes, unless they are lucky enough to get a little fuel through the black market. And then it costs them a fortune. Thank goodness my family is in the good old U.S.A. These countries are all the same honey, I want no part of any of them. I just want to get back home to you.

Tues nite 10:30 pm
6 Feb 1945

The 14th is Valentine's Day, so I'm sending you this money order. It's not much my Valentine, but get something real nice for yourself. Just finished seeing a show here at the billets, Humphrey Bogart in 'To have or Have Not' I think was the name of it. And it was very good. An order came out today stating that leaves and furloughs were in effect the first of feb. That is if you want to go to England. I won't put in for one because I want to spend any possible furlough with just you. I haven't had any time off since I've been across, almost fifteen months now. It would sure be grand if I could be home before I'm in the army two years. Just pray my darling and keep your fingers crossed. When this thing is over my darling I'm going to get down on my knees and thank God.

ACKNOWLEDGMENTS

THE LENGTH OF THIS list leaves me deeply humbled.

Thank you to my book team: to my incredible editor, Pamela Feinsilber, the sanity to my madness, the safety net under my tightrope, the wizard behind the curtain. For saying yes without hesitation and being there at all hours with your generous heart. You are a powerhouse, and our conversations have been an important learning journey for me.

To my brilliant designer, Jacqueline Gilman, for giving my dream structure and foundation—you are the alchemist and I'm beyond grateful to you. To Drew Foerster, for your cover design and for delivering my constant changes with joy and ease. Your commitment to everything you touch is a reflection of your wildly generous heart and has meant the world to me. You have made this book and the last several years of the letters-project pitches possible.

Big love and thanks to my publicist, Heather Besignano, and my badass team at Icon PR, Alexis Pappas and Julia Westerhout.

To my UK agent, Miles Anthony, for your friendship and love of a good story. To my team at CAA: Robert Mickelson, Katie Laner, Rick Roskin, Norris Brooks, and Rob Light. And to Irving Azoff, for always looking out for me.

To my family at the Garry Marshall Theatre, where much of this book was written: Heather Hall, Barbara Marshall, Kathleen Marshall, and Lori Marshall, thank you for generously sharing your book team with me and cheering me on. And to Garry, my guardian angel, for giving me my first professional writing jobs and the confidence to know I could fulfill my lifelong dream of becoming a published author. Tom Hanks and Paula Wagner, for always being there for me with such generosity of spirit and advice. And Mr. Ron Howard, for reminding me that my power is on the page. To my creative soulmate, Aditya Patwardhan, thank you for everything you are. You've stuck with me through all the lifetimes, and now, we've got a movie to make.

To the beautiful souls who gave me the honor of reading my memoir before it was published: Bette Midler, Patty Jenkins, John Patrick Shanley, Melissa Roxburgh, Alexander Vlahos, Joe Mantegna, Jeff Garlin, Gray Fagan, Haley Joel Osment, Justin Willman, Dean Norris, Samiyah Swann, Bailey Wax, Lisa Stanley, Loni Love. Each of you hold an incredibly special place in my heart.

Deepest thanks to my investors—Matt Burns, Mark Ian Burnstein, and Marla and Kirk Daily—for joining the Remember Me As Human team without hesitation and totally believing in me and the project. You are the miracle makers, and the world needs more of you. I will pass it on in your honor, and in memory of Alex Burnstein.

To the many people who said no: You guided me to those who said yes. You forced me to become more creative in my thinking and more resourceful than I ever imagined I could be; thank you for that.

Love and gratitude to friends and family who

patiently put up with me over the past ten years as I wrote this book, providing notes and feedback no matter how many times I asked—you know who you are, and I owe you many favors. Rachel Montez Minor, for your loving guidance from two steps ahead. To Tim and Talor Ray, for your deep love and for hosting, driving, and feeding me on my research/writing trips to Illinois. To Donna and Mike Reed, Sandy Moses, Connie Boyer, and Doug and Jana Boyer, for your factual help and kind support.

To the staff at Newman Rehabilitation and Health Care Center, thank you and respect for your hard work and for continuing to keep Wanda Mae's memory alive. To Margie Hinrichs, for being so gracious when a total stranger knocked on your door to ask about her Roughton ancestors who used to live on your land. To Rich and Lynn Holm, for graciously allowing us Boyers to visit your home, a place that has meant so much to us, and for taking the farm into the future with your own family legacy.

To dearest Dr. Daniel Ryan, thank you for channeling my loved ones on the other side as they guided me through to the book's completion. And to that heavenly cheer squad, led by Uncle Mickey: As you've reminded me from spirit, this story belongs to us all, and WE DID IT! And foremost, thank you to Grandma Wanda and Grandpa Dale for being the inspiration behind it all. It has been my heart's most fervent desire to keep your memories alive, and I can breathe easier now.

Deepest gratitude to my parents, Jody and Jim Recor and Joe Walsh. Mom, thank you for giving me the world, and for honoring me with your trust as I wrote about you and your family. Jim Dad, you are the wind beneath my wings, eternally. Dad, for being my greatest teacher in this life. I love the three of you more than life itself. Grace Guindon and Spencer Recor, you are my everything.

To my husband, William Sweeny: Your unwavering love is my life raft in this tumultuous ocean. Thank you for selflessly supporting my creative ideas, as I regularly go off by myself and use much of our money to achieve them, with such trust. I'm here for your incredible talents the same, always.

And to the reader, for sharing this space with me and celebrating our humanity together. I love you. Thank you.

ABOUT THE AUTHOR

LUCY WALSH IS AN award-winning actress and musician, appearing in films (Garry Marshall's *Mother's Day*) and plays (Shakespeare's *Antony and Cleopatra* and *The Tempest*) and on television (*Curb Your Enthusiasm, NCIS, Criminal Minds*). She has toured internationally with her music, most recently with Maroon 5 and One Republic. Her song "Winter Coat" is on the *Mother's Day* soundtrack; her cover version of "Not Alone Anymore" is on the *Roy Orbison: Under the Covers* album. She also composed the score for the 2022 film *Normal* and is featured on Billy Bob Thornton's musical film project *And Then We Drove*. Most recently, however, she has focused on writing. *Remember Me as Human* is her first book. Currently working on a screenplay based on the letters her grandparents exchanged during World War II, Walsh divides her time between New York and England with her husband, William Sweeny, and their two cats, Gilbert and Jessica Daisy Bing Bings.

Printed in the USA
CPSIA information can be obtained
at www.ICGtesting.com
LVHW042008100424
776966LV00002B/313